THE
BOOK
OF

Faeries

THE
BOOK
OF
Faeries

A guide to the world of elves, pixies, goblins, and other magic spirits

Francis Melville

FAIR WINDS

P R E S S

A QUARTO BOOK

10 9 8 7 6 5 4 3 2 1

ISBN 1- 931412-03-0

Fair Winds Press
33 Commercial Street
Gloucester, MA 01930
USA

Sheridan House
112–116A Western Road
Hove
East Sussex BN3 1DD
England

Copyright © 2002 Quarto Publishing plc

Conceived, designed, and produced by
Quarto Publishing plc
The Old Brewery
6 Blundell Street
London N7 9BH

QUAR.WING

Senior editor: Michelle Pickering
Art editor: Jill Mumford
Assistant art director: Penny Cobb
Designer: Julie Francis
Illustrators: Veronica Aldous, Greg Becker,
Janie Coath, Elsa Godfrey, Griselda
Holderness, Martin Jones, Olivia Rayner,
Rob Sheffield
Indexer: Dorothy Frame

Art director: Moira Clinch
Publisher: Piers Spence

Manufactured by Regent Publishing
Services Ltd, Hong Kong
Printed by Midas Printing Ltd, China

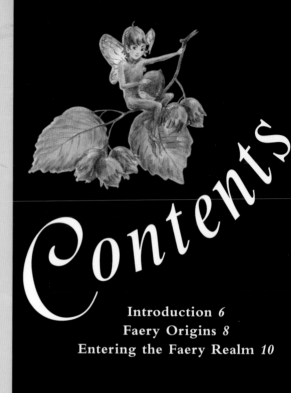

Contents

Introduction

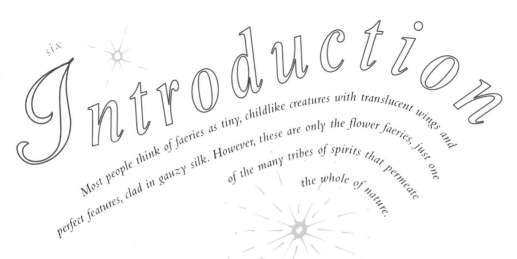

Most people think of faeries as tiny, childlike creatures with translucent wings and perfect features, clad in gauzy silk. However, these are only the flower faeries, just one of the many tribes of spirits that permeate the whole of nature.

It is an astonishing fact that every culture in the world shares a traditional belief in the existence of the "little people." Faeries are generally believed to be a diverse race of spiritual beings that manifest in anthropomorphic form as smaller, often oddly shaped versions of humans. There is also an extraordinary correlation between faeries' roles and activities and those of human beings. Every human society that works metals or precious stones, for example, has a shared belief in dwarfish beings who live in the mountains and are expert miners and metalworkers.

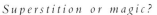

Superstition or magic?

Modern western cultures tend to dismiss these traditional beliefs as quaint folk tales generated by simple, superstitious minds. In psychology, tales of faeries are perceived as fantasies projected from the emotional subconscious, or archetypes of the collective human unconscious. However, many people around the world continue to believe that there is a magical side of life that has been all but forgotten in the three-dimensional, sense-orientated modern world.

The faery realm

So where are faeries to be found? The answer is that they inhabit the same world as humans, but their existence has a fourth dimension that frees them from the confines of time and space. Inhabitants of the faery realm are therefore not bound by the same material laws. While humans must face the inevitability, if not the finality, of death, faeries are usually immortal, hence the Celtic name for the faery realm, Tir Na N'Og—the land of the ever young. The Greeks called it Hesperides, meaning the blessed isles, and in Arthurian romance, it is the isle of Avalon. It is always considered separate from the world of humans, but either connected by water or contained within the earth itself.

A world of enchantment

This book explores the folklore of some of the most important faery tribes, describing their characteristics and activities and exploring ways of interacting with them. Just allow the wonder of creation to fill your mind, and with a little bit of luck, you can enjoy the friendship of a faery and bring enchantment to your world.

Faery Origins

Faeries are part of the great mystery of life, and to believe in them is more enchanting and satisfying than to dismiss them for lack of hard evidence. Over the course of time, various theories have been expounded to explain their existence.

One theory is that faeries are former deities whose power and influence have dwindled, as reflected in their diminutive size. Another theory holds that faeries are the spirits of the dead—the word sprite, meaning faery, is derived from spirit.

Angelic beginnings

A belief common to Christian, Islamic, and to a certain extent Jewish traditions tells us that the little people are of angelic origin. In the great war of heaven, Satan, swollen with vainglorious pride, refused to submit to God's authority and led a third of the angels into a titanic struggle with the angels of light, who were led by the archangel Michael. Defeated, the rebellious angels were cast from heaven into the material world. The faery tribes are supposed to be lesser angels that somehow managed to get caught up on the wrong side and were evicted from heaven with the fallen angels.

Those faeries who were not embittered by their fall from grace made the most of their new habitat and delighted in the fascinating workings of nature. They look to

mankind as part of their salvation, through the creation of an
earthly paradise that will bring redemption to all. Some faeries,
however, hid in the dark recesses of the earth, licking their
wounds. They hold humans partly responsible for their fate,
since one of Satan's sins was refusing to bow down before
humanity. This explains their antipathy toward people and
provides their main motivation.

Pygmy natives

A tradition common to the Celts and other roving peoples
of the world is that the little people were pygmy natives
of the lands they moved into. These faeries took refuge
in the hills, finding entrances to the hollow earth. They
do not trust humans, but they are sufficiently intrigued
by our strange doings to pay us some attention and
even mimic or participate in some of our activities.

Devic nature spirits

A race of faery entities that does not fit into
any of these theories is the devas. These
spirits are responsible for all the processes
and functions of the natural world.
Their identities are entirely related
to their work and they have no
moral responses.

nine

Entering the Faery Realm

Learning to embrace the faery realm requires an open mind and a generous spirit. A childlike innocence and sense of wonder help, as do an enthusiastic and fertile imagination and an appreciation of the beauty and mysteriousness of nature.

Faeries are spiritual beings and intelligent energies that, although they do not have material bodies, can manifest in any form they wish. Like humans, they are capable of evolving and developing as individuals, according to their experience of life. However, despite this important similarity and the fact that they exist in the same world as we do, the faery realm remains invisible to most of us.

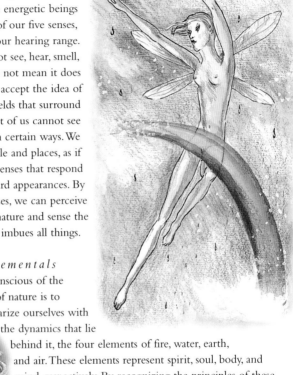

Developing intuition

The frequencies at which these energetic beings function are beyond the reach of our five senses, just as certain sounds lie outside our hearing range. However, just because we cannot see, hear, smell, touch, or taste something, does not mean it does not exist. Many people now accept the idea of auras, those subtle energetic fields that surround our bodies. Even though most of us cannot see them, we can sense them in certain ways. We receive impressions about people and places, as if instinctively, using subtle senses that respond to much more than outward appearances. By developing these intuitive senses, we can perceive the intelligences that animate nature and sense the secret glory that imbues all things.

Connecting with the elementals

Another way to become more conscious of the secret life of nature is to familiarize ourselves with the dynamics that lie behind it, the four elements of fire, water, earth, and air. These elements represent spirit, soul, body, and mind, respectively. By recognizing the principles of these elements as they work within ourselves, we can become more aware of our own being and hence more in tune with everything around us.

The four elemental spirits—salamanders, sylphs, gnomes, and undines—can act as portals into the faery realm. On pages 14–21 you will find ideas of how to connect with them. By doing so, you will become less self-conscious and self-absorbed. You can then become attuned to the presence of other, more subtle entities. Let us step into their world.

eleven

CHAPTER ONE

Elementals & Nature Spirits

The whole of nature is teeming with spirits. In fact, nothing can happen in nature without the attention of the elementals and devas. Elementals are concerned with the elemental processes of fire, water, earth, and air, while devas attend to every aspect of plant life, from seed germination to flowering. In addition, there are many other nature spirits, from the elves that guard wild places to the ice spirit Jack Frost.

Salamanders
elementals

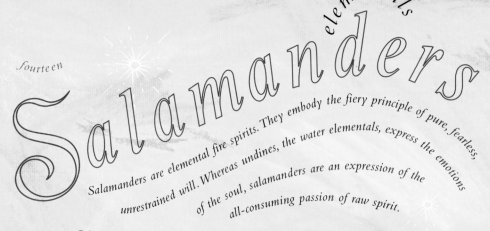

Salamanders are elemental fire spirits. They embody the fiery principle of pure, fearless, unrestrained will. Whereas undines, the water elementals, express the emotions of the soul, salamanders are an expression of the all-consuming passion of raw spirit.

Salamanders are nature's pyrotechnicians, exploring every aspect of fire, from the magma at the molten core of the earth to the electricity of a lightning bolt. Their quest is to connect with the secret fire that lies at the heart of all things in the natural world.

Danger of combustion

Salamanders are the most highly charged and dangerous of all the elemental spirits. They are dangerous not because they are malevolently disposed toward humans but because they are so far removed from our level of being. To commune with salamanders is to risk total destruction. Any fears or unresolved emotions can combust like gasoline in the white-hot presence of a salamander. To identify with any negativity is to stand like a dead pine in the face of a forest fire.

However, humans can learn a great deal from salamanders. Fire is the primary element that acts upon the others, turning solids into liquids and liquids into gases by the action of its heat. The sun is the material reflection of the divine fire. Its light and heat provide the vital dynamic acting upon our planet. Salamanders were born when the first volcano spewed forth the vast amounts of vapor that established the atmosphere and oceans, which in turn provided the matrix for planetary life. They have been exploring the transforming nature of fire ever since.

Holding a fire ritual

Begin by focusing on the flame of a candle. Close your eyes and think about the internal obstacles that hinder your development. Visualize each one combusting into flames. Imagine the fire melting the stones in your heart and vaporizing the heavy waters of emotional pain and turmoil inside you. Next, see the passion in your heart igniting and let it fill and expand your spirit, raising you above your former limitations. When sufficiently lightened and purified, you can partake in the salamanders' wild and joyful exultations and share their quest to unite with the secret fire at the heart of nature.

Sylphs elementals

Sylphs are the rulers of the sky, the elemental spirits of air. They are graceful and feminine but as wild as the winds they stir, as free as the birds they bear aloft, and as passionate and capricious as the weather they help create.

Sylphs are endowed with all the qualities of the element air. They sigh on the breeze that hisses through cornfields, whisper on winds that rustle through trees, whip up the dust devils that presage a sandstorm, and shriek with the gales that lash the great seas. In summer, they slumber on languorous air, heavy with perfume and the buzzing of bees.

Spirits of inspiration

Although sylphs can be tempestuous, essentially they are light, harmonious, expressive, and inspirational. To commune with a sylph is to experience amazing clarity of vision, enabling you to view the world with the crisp focus of an eagle, while the inner eye of your intellect sees things as they really are. Air is also the medium of hearing and smelling, since sounds and scents are carried by the air. Sylphs are highly musical, creating wonderful symphonies from all the sounds that are borne on the breeze. To listen to the sylphs' melodies is to be inspired—literally, for the word inspire comes from the Latin inspirare, meaning to breathe in. They breathe inspiration into us, connecting us with the great mind they inhabit, for just as the element earth represents the body, water the soul, and fire the spirit, air represents the mind.

Playing with sylphs

To share the experience of a sylph, go outside, away from the noises of city streets. Relax into your breathing and listen for the sound of the air talking through trees. Feel its caress against your cheeks. Open your arms and spread yourself upon the breeze, allowing it to carry you, spiraling up like a summer thermal or rolling across hills. Sense the freedom, the pleasure of unrestricted being. Let yourself go and the sylphs will come and play with you. They may show you how they make crop circles, or even take you to a wild party in the sky, where they join forces with salamanders to create ecstatic thunderstorms.

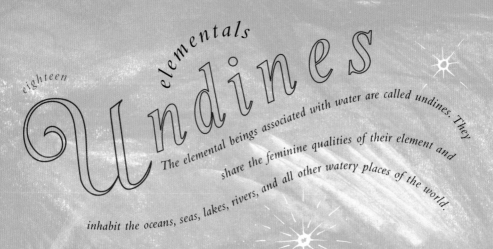

elementals
Undines

The elemental beings associated with water are called undines. They share the feminine qualities of their element and inhabit the oceans, seas, lakes, rivers, and all other watery places of the world.

Water is psychic and intuitive like its ruler, the moon. It has a connecting, magnetic quality to it. It conducts sounds and currents, and has powers of mediation and communication. Undines are therefore the most empathetic of the elemental beings and many people find them the easiest to relate to.

Invoking your undine soul mate

To be with an undine is to be intimately known and cherished. All you have to do is let go and flow. Think water, be water. Imagine yourself as a drop of rain falling from a cloud into a fast-flowing river. As soon as you hit the surface, you are caught in the flow and suddenly there she is, an undine, embracing you, feeling you, knowing you, loving you, merging with you. Together you are the body of water, stretching and twisting, writhing around boulders, throwing up rainbows as you splash over waterfalls. You feel every texture, every contour of the banks and riverbed that shape your rushing course. Never have you felt such a wonderful sense of release. All your emotions and feelings flow unabated, unashamed, and understood. All the fresh, clean, limpid, purifying qualities of water saturate your being with a thrilling, sensual ecstasy.

Gradually the pace of the current starts to slacken. You and your undine spin lazily in pools and eddies as she communicates to you the secrets of all the places that the water has explored on its journey. As you reach the great ocean, you merge with vast currents and sink into the velvet darkness. Here, you are initiated into the primordial wisdom of the deep. This is the source, where life first expressed itself, where the first cell divided in the watery womb of mother earth. Here, there can be no loneliness, no separation, for here all is one, all is love. Buoyed by this awareness, you rise toward the light. You say goodbye to your undine soul mate as the sun draws you up into the air.

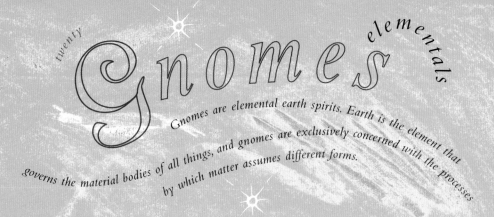

Gnomes

elementals

Gnomes are elemental earth spirits. Earth is the element that governs the material bodies of all things, and gnomes are exclusively concerned with the processes by which matter assumes different forms.

A gnome's main sphere of interest is the mineral world. Gnomes do not govern the formation of metals and minerals—that is the work of the mineral devas—but they seek to understand how the building blocks of physical life work. This is why alchemists and magicians have always sought their assistance. Alchemists wish to penetrate the very nature of matter in order to manipulate and exalt it. Magicians want to know how atoms combine to create forms so that they can conjure things from thin air and increase their power over nature.

Diamond watchers

Gnomes are, naturally, very down-to-earth. They are serious, practical, industrious, critical, single-minded, and patient. Magicians use elaborate rituals and incantations to summon and command gnomes to do their will. Gnomes evoked in this way have the appearance of tiny, wizened old men with weak eyes and narrow, pointed noses.

Gnomes that have been summoned against their will appear taciturn and grumpy because they hate being dragged into our time and space, which is very uncomfortable for

them. They operate at much lower frequencies than humans. What seems to us an eon is just a short time to gnomes. They can inhabit the space between atoms and patiently observe a lump of coal turning into a diamond.

Communing with gnomes

To commune with gnomes, you need to slow yourself down to their frequencies by practicing meditation. When you have achieved a state of great stillness, focus your attention on descending deep into the heart of matter. If you can become sufficiently profound while remaining alert, you may encounter a gnome on his own ground. There, he is neither sulky nor slow. He is bright, sharp, and brimming with enthusiasm. He takes delight in the interest of humans, and if you ask the right questions, he will be happy to share his knowledge. He will be able to explain how lead turns into gold in the crucible of the earth.

Devas

nature spirits

Devas are the spirits that hold nature together.
Everything manifest in the universe has an idea behind it, a thought form that
is the blueprint of a physical form. Devas ensure that these thought
forms are made manifest.

While biologists are still trying to find out how matter created life, ancient tradition affirms that life created matter. In the beginning there was consciousness. Consciousness is the need to be. In order to satisfy this need, consciousness created life, and in order to evolve, life created matter.

Organizing intelligences

The word deva means god or divinity in Sanskrit. Devas are the shining ones of Buddhist and Hindu tradition, sentient spiritual beings, like angels, that act as the organizing intelligences for everything that exists. It is they who are responsible for the so-called evolution of nature. When William Blake, in his famous poem, asks of the tiger "What immortal hand or eye could frame thy fearful symmetry?" the answer is the tiger deva manifesting an idea formed in the mind of nature.

Everything has its spirit

Devas are the vitalizing spiritual mirror of the material world. They provide matter with organization and cohesion. Every atom and molecule has its spirit, without which it would have no cohesion. Devas are the glue that binds the fabric of the universe together. Every individual being has its own deva, which acts as its instinctual mechanism. This provides the tiger with its instinct to survive and ensures that everything it absorbs from food turns into tiger. Every species of tiger has its own deva, while a higher deva presides over tigers in general, and an even higher deva over the whole cat family. A yet higher deva presides over all mammals and so on. In the plant kingdom it is the devas that preside over the activities of the flower faeries and other lesser plant spirits.

Unlimited potential

Devas are spirits that are able to evolve over time. As they sense the relationship of their current function to higher functions, they can take on ever greater tasks. For example, when a mineral molecule is absorbed by a plant root, it becomes part of the plant. The molecule's deva can then become a root deva. As it realizes the relationship of the roots with the rest of the plant, it can then evolve into a leaf faery or flower faery. If it should become aware of a gardener's appreciation of its flower, it might become a deva connected to the art of gardening, for devas also make up the spirit behind all arts, crafts, communities, and nations, as well as buildings, cities, rivers, and mountains. Everything is connected and it is the devas that forge the connections. There is no limit to a deva's potential. It can go on to become a great archangel, just as we humans can aspire to ever greater consciousness.

Devas as teachers

In the late 1960s, during the earliest days of the famous Findhorn community in Scotland, Dorothy Maclean received instructions from plant devas while in deep meditation. She and her colleagues carried out these instructions and produced a miraculously fertile and abundant garden in a virtual desert of sand dunes, producing specimens of extraordinary size and vigor.

Horticultural experts came from all over the world to confirm this miracle for themselves. Ever since, the knowledge of plant devas has spread around the globe.

Devas were always there, of course, and had been known of in the past, but we in the modern world had all but forgotten their existence. In traditional societies, those able to perceive and work with these spirits are known as shamans and medicine men. In the past there were also witches, wise women, and alchemists who worked with devas, but they were persecuted by the ruthless enforcers of religious and scientific dogma, who were either fearful of the spiritual world or in denial of its existence.

We can all have green fingers

You do not have to have special powers to communicate with plant devas. By simply acknowledging their existence, and approaching plants with greater wonder and reverence, you can start to learn, as if by intuition, some of their secrets. As your relationship develops, more information can be communicated according to your particular interests, be they medicinal, nutritional, or horticultural. In the Rituals & Recipes chapter at the end of this book you will find more about how to establish communication with the devas and work with them.

Flower Faeries

nature spirits

Ask anyone to describe a faery and they will most likely describe a flower faery—tiny, slender, and childlike with diaphanous wings. Flower faeries are plant spirits whose coloring and clothing match the flowers that they tend.

Tiny and graceful with gauzy dragonfly wings, flower faeries have the delightful task of tending to the blooms of all the flowering plants of the world. Under the rulership of the devas, the ruling spirits of nature, they work ceaselessly throughout the day to make sure that their flowers produce the right colors, scents, and organs to attract insects and ensure successful pollination.

The Cottingley faeries

In 1917 two girls claimed that they had seen faeries playing in a glen at Cottingley in the north of England. The famous photographs they took appear to show flower faeries in the presence of the girls. Many eminent people of the day argued that the photographs were a hoax, while others, such as Sherlock Holmes creator Sir Arthur Conan Doyle, argued passionately that they were authentic. Although the girls eventually admitted that the photographs were indeed a hoax, they maintained until their deaths that they really had seen faeries.

Cicely Mary Barker

The most enchanting depictions of flower faeries are those painted by Cicely Mary Barker in the 1920s, which are still in print today. Each faery is shown with its host plant and is accompanied by a verse describing the plant's habits and characteristics. The dazzling vivacity of both image and verse continues to delight children and adults alike.

Seeing a flower faery

Dressed in the same apparel as their flowers, these faeries are among the easiest of the faery folk to visualize and actually see. The best time to do so is between sunrise and midday when they are engaged in the opening of flowers and the attraction of insects. You cannot see them by looking at them directly, but those darting, shimmering lights that you sometimes catch out of the corner of your eye ... well, who can say what they really are.

Nymphs

Nymphs are female spirits who inhabit places of great natural beauty. They represent the pure, unspoiled, feminine aspect of nature and invariably appear as beautiful, nubile maidens.

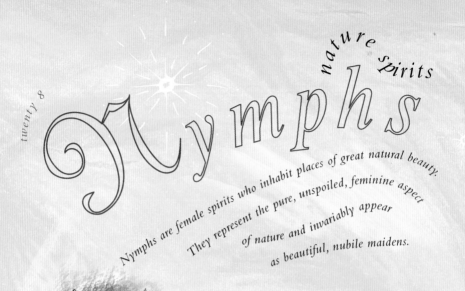

Nymphs are rarely more than semi-clad, and this nakedness reflects their innocence and lack of self-consciousness. Nymphs exist all over the world, but it is around the Mediterranean Sea that you are most likely to see or sense them. Mediterranean people have always been particularly well-attuned to the nymphs' unique energies, and have enjoyed many encounters with them. The several types of nymph are all similar in appearance, yet each has very different functions. All are deemed handmaidens of the nature goddess Diana.

Dryads and oreads

Dryads are the guardian spirits of trees and woods. Their name is derived from druas, the Greek word for oak, the ruling tree of the forest. The mountains belong to the oreads, who are closely connected with Aphrodite, goddess of love. The oreads are passionate and, despite their natural shyness, are often amorously inclined toward humans. Their coy sensuality contrasts with the lasciviousness of their male counterparts, the goat-legged fauns and satyrs.

Naiads and other water nymphs

Nymphs have always congregated near water. Inhabiting freshwater springs and streams are the naiads, who ensure that the pools remain full of water during hot summers. They work in harmony with dryads, whose trees shade the naiads' pools, and ensure that the springs continue to slake the thirst of plants and animals alike. The nymphs' own survival depends on these pools, for they are not necessarily immortal and may perish if their springs dry up or if their trees die. Naiad-protected waters have always been considered sacred. Some have healing properties, and others are known to inspire oracular or mystical visions and are revered as holy shrines.

Naiads feature frequently in classical Greek literature. The most beautiful was said to be Aegle, and it was her union with the sun god Helios that produced the three graces or charities. Another, called Salmakis, fell so passionately in love with Hermaphroditus, the son of Hermes and Aphrodite, that she pulled him into her pool, where their bodies merged into one.

The other main groups of water nymph are the oceanids and nereids. Oceanids inhabit the great oceans, while nereids, who sometimes take the form of mermaids, live in the Mediterranean Sea and help sailors in danger of shipwreck or drowning.

How to see a nymph

You might be lucky enough to encounter a nymph in a place of exceptional natural beauty. However, you will not find them by looking for them. The trick is to be as enchanted by the loveliness of the trees, rocks, and springs as the

nymphs are themselves. They delight in our appreciation, which, if fine enough, can cause them to frolic joyfully around us. Warm, sunny afternoons are the most likely moments to sense them and rejoice in their magical presence.

twenty 9

Fauns & Satyrs

nature spirits

Among the most colorful of all the nature spirits are the fauns and satyrs so celebrated in classical times. They serve the great god Pan, the spirit of nature, and protect the wildlife of the woods and fields.

Fauns and satyrs appear as small, goat-legged men with curled horns and cloven hooves. As attendants of Bacchus, the god of wine, their lives are a constant celebration of the wild fertility and bounty of nature. They are the hell-raisers of the faery kingdom, with a reputation for drunkenness, lechery, and lewdness. They spend their time dancing and playing panpipes, and are always in amorous pursuit of nymphs.

Ancient Greece and Rome

In ancient Greece, performances of theatrical tragedies often had bawdy interludes or post-plays featuring satyrs—this is the origin of the satire play. On Greek and Roman ceramics, fauns and satyrs are often portrayed parading around with enormous erections, and their infectious lust for life inspired the famous Roman bacchanalia—drunken midsummer orgies involving thousands of people that were held in the open countryside.

Frolicking in the wild places

Nowadays we are most unlikely to encounter a faun or satyr because they no longer have any interest in human beings. Although they used to befriend humans, and took delight in teasing and playing pranks on us, they now see us as traitors, vandals, and party-poopers. As individuals, however, we have no need to fear them, particularly if we treat their environment with reverence and share their indomitable love of life. Their spirit is still alive in the wild places, but the days when they used to frolic among us belong to a distant age.

nature spirits
Elves

Of all the faery folk, the elves are the most steeped in romantic legend. There was a time when the word elf was used to denote all manner of spiritual beings, but it has since come to refer to a specific class of little people who are the guardians of wild places.

Elves are creatures of light, known to the Irish as the Tuatha Dé Danann, the people of Dana, the mother earth goddess. She entrusted the elves as custodians of nature, overseeing the work of the nature devas and delighting in the beauty of the natural world and all the creatures that inhabit it.

The fair folk

Elves are often called the fair folk, being finer in every way than ourselves. With their softly slanted eyes and sharp features, they epitomize natural grace and intelligence. Elves are so highly attuned spiritually that their bodies are less dense than ours. This allows them to shape-shift, to fly through the air, and even to pass through solid objects.

Elves are also known as trooping faeries, which means that they live in a community rather than as solitary individuals. Theirs is the romantic ideal of society, a perfect hierarchy headed by a king and queen. Their whole life is a ritual of love. They celebrate the seasons and the forces of nature, dancing and frolicking throughout the night around their

faery fires that burn with a bluish
light that neither scorches nor
consumes. They are seldom
seen in daylight, not because
they shun the light but
because the sun's rays
shine through them.
They are not dense
enough to cast a shadow.

Appreciating nature

Although elves are naturally
well-disposed toward humans,
their relationship with us has become
increasingly strained. They
honor humankind, knowing
that our great mission is to
express the soul of the planet just as they
express its spirit, but they grieve at our
ignorance and viciousness and have become
wary of us. Some find it hard to forgive us our trespasses
against nature and shun us. However, those humans
who possess "the sight" may still see elves, as can anyone
whose lightness of being and alert appreciation of nature
approaches theirs. Signs of their presence include the
so-called faery rings, those mysterious circles of little
mushrooms where the elves hold their ritual revels.

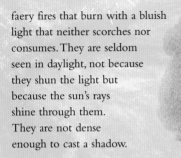

thirty 3

Tree Spirits

Trees are quite literally teeming with faery life. Just as they shelter birds and other wildlife, trees are also host to numerous faery tribes, including leaf and flower faeries, devas and soul spirits, and various guardian spirits.

Leaf and flower faeries attend to the tree's foliage and fertility, while the deva of each species determines its overall growth pattern. Each tree also has its own soul spirit, which is born when the tree germinates and passes on when it dies. All of these faeries help to give a tree its unique personality, which explains why some trees are aloof and forbidding while others invite us to climb up and play in their spreading branches.

The radande, dryads, and hamadryads

Trees are also home to faeries that act as guardian spirits—the radande, dryads, and hamadryads. The radande are one of several tribes of woodland faeries of Swedish folklore. Each tree has its own ra, a spirit that can move around its host. It readily bestows favors on those who respect it, ensuring good crops of fruit and nuts.

Dryads and hamadryads are sometimes perceived as beautiful females from the waist up, while their lower parts embody the trunk and roots. Dryads are able to move from tree to tree at will and often congregate in the oldest and strongest trees, whereas hamadryads are inextricably attached to their host tree. The radande and hamadryads depend entirely on their trees for their vitality, dying with their hosts.

Looking for faery trees

Every culture has its own sacred trees where the most powerful spirits reside. For example, in the ancient faery land of Albion (now Britain), oak, ash, and hawthorn are favorite faery haunts. When looking for faery trees, seek out the oldest and most healthy specimens. These are the tribal elders. Sit down and rest your back against the trunk. While absorbing the tree's vitalizing energy, allow its spirits to share their secrets with you. As always, gentleness and respect will allow you to commune with the faery realm.

If you ever need to cut a tree down, always ask the old boss tree first and explain your need. It will help you to select the right tree, one that is ready to be cut, and allow any spirits who can to leave.

Corn Spirit

The corn spirit is a deva, one of the ruling nature spirits. We depend on her for the fertility of the grain and a successful harvest each year—the better we treat the soil and the more respect we show the corn spirit, the more vital and nutritious the crop.

The corn spirit has been revered around the world since humankind first began harvesting grain. North American Indians, such as the Cherokee, honored the corn spirit as well as spirits for other types of crop. Like all nature spirits, the corn spirit is weakened by modern practices such as the use of pesticides.

The ritual of the corn sheaf

Before the advent of mechanical harvesters, farming communities conducted many annual rituals to honor the corn spirit. She was believed to hide in the last sheaf of corn to be cut at harvest time, so this would be set aside and then ceremoniously carried into the tithe barn, where a wreath would be woven from it. The head of the community would take the wreath and hang it in a place of honor in the church. Come midwinter, some of the sheaf would be fed to the cows to ensure good calving and a generous milk yield. The rest would be woven into a corn dolly and left in the barn to protect the fertility and nutrition of the grain. Later, it would be plowed under the earth to secure a good harvest the following year.

Making a tall spiral sheaf

Soak five wheat straws in cool water for 30 minutes, then wrap them in a towel for 15 minutes. Tie the straws together with cotton thread just below the grains. Lay the sheaf out flat so that the straws form a cross, with one of the arms made by two straws.

Begin weaving by taking one of the two straws and folding it over the straw next to it, parallel to the next arm of the cross. Taking that arm, bend it around the new one and fold it over so that it is parallel to the third arm, and so on. Once the first round is complete, you should have a square. Continue weaving in this manner, increasing the width of the corn dolly's spiral until the desired size is achieved. When you reach the neck of the dolly, braid the remaining straws together and tie them in a loop.

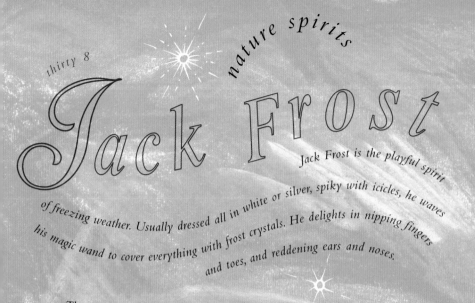

Jack Frost

Jack Frost is the playful spirit of freezing weather. Usually dressed all in white or silver, spiky with icicles, he waves his magic wand to cover everything with frost crystals. He delights in nipping fingers and toes, and reddening ears and noses.

There are few things more transporting than waking on a late fall morning to find the world transformed by frost into a dazzling winter wonderland with flashing, sparkling, gently tinkling ice crystals festooning every grass blade, every twig. Children especially cannot wait to get their coats, boots, and gloves on and run out into the splendor of it all.

The cold air catches in your throat and makes you gasp. Your eyes gleam and your face stretches into a great grin of sheer wonderment and joy. Frosted leaves crunch beneath your boots. You pick one up and gaze, amazed, at the delicate, lacy intricacy of the pattern, every tiny vein picked out in pearly silver gauze like faery wings.

The icy imp

What conjuror has wrought this wonder? Jack Frost, of course—who else! The imp of ice has been working through the night to brighten up the dreary march of winter. He uses those early winter nights when the sky clears and the temperature plummets to condense the damp air into tiny ice crystals that form on every surface. If the air is very still, the crystals interlock and form beautiful shapes of astonishing intricacy that resemble ferns and flowers. As the sun comes up, the countless crystal surfaces reflect and refract the sunlight, flashing like a million priceless gems. The tiniest breath of wind causes a tinkling cascade.

You can almost hear Jack's laughter as grown-ups lose their dignity, slipping on the ice. His icy fingers nip at ears and noses. Cover up well and keep on the move or Jack will show you just how cold his heart is. He will creep into the marrow of your bones and suck your very life out if you let him, for his mistress is the Snow Queen, the cruel and icy heart of winter. Enjoy Jack's dazzling carnival of frost, but beware thin ice and tend your inner fire.

Jack-in-the-Green

Also known as the green man, Jack-in-the-green is the spirit of the greenwood, whose counterparts are revered and celebrated throughout Europe in all the areas that were once densely wooded with deciduous trees.

Jack-in-the-green represents the eternal return of spring following the death of fall and the decay of winter. This annual miracle is most graphically expressed by the eruption of green vegetation from the bare earth. Jack-in-the-green is celebrated ritually at spring festivals, represented either by a man dressed in green clothes or a wire cage covered in leafy vegetation. The green man's image, with vegetation coiling around his head, is also found adorning the architecture and wooden pews of many medieval churches.

Robin Hood

Legendary folk heroes of the greenwood, such as Robin Hood and the green knight of Arthurian legend, are characters inspired by this nature spirit. There may have been a historical figure around whom the legends of Robin Hood coiled like bindweed, but in essence Robin and his merry men represent the ancient spirit of the woodlands. Dressed in green and hiding in the forest, they are the laughter in the woods, delighting in outfoxing and punishing the conquering Normans, usurpers of their ancestral land. In this respect they are a metaphor for the faeries and other little people who have withdrawn into the wildwood to hide from humans. Like Robin Hood, Jack-in-the-green is a cunning trickster who delights in playing pranks on humans, punishing those who show disrespect for natural law.

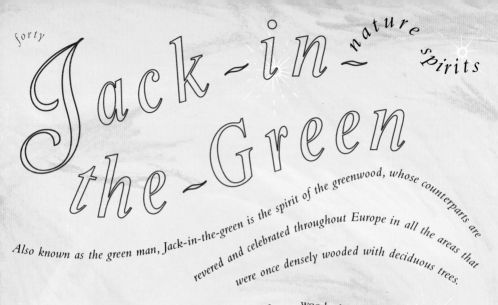

Feeling Jack's energy

The exuberant spirit of Jack-in-the-green can be felt whenever we abandon our humdrum selves and plunge into the greening woods in spring or early summer. When you do so, listen out for Jack's familiar, the laughing green woodpecker. As you listen to its distinctive call, close your eyes and share the revitalizing energy that is coursing through the earth. Allow it to enter your toes and rise up through your body.

CHAPTER TWO

Faery Helpers

Not all faeries have specific functions in the natural world. Some of these unemployed little people have become sufficiently interested in the activities of humans to share our homes and imitate our behavior. Although many have retained their innate sense of mischievous fun, when treated with tact and respect they can be very useful co-workers, and some can greatly enhance our lives by sharing the mysteries of certain crafts.

Brownies

Brownies are generally described as shaggy, little, brown-skinned, dark-haired men, up to 3 feet (1 meter) tall. They are particularly well-known in Britain, especially northern England and Scotland, where the name originates.

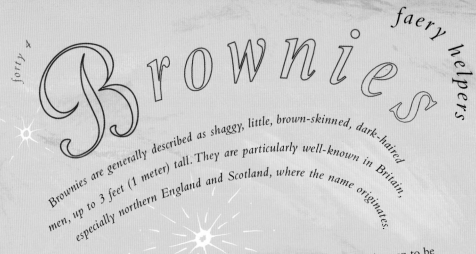

Many people used to believe that brownies were the aboriginal inhabitants of Britain before the arrival of the Celts. Although there is evidence that these people were smaller in stature than the Celts, it is much more likely that brownies are one of the faery folk rather than pygmy humans.

Habits and customs

There is a wealth of lore pertaining to these elusive little people. They are generally solitary and attach themselves to households, particularly farms and country houses, although they occasionally develop a special attachment to a family and follow them when they move. They perform all manner of chores, including laborious farm work such as mowing and threshing corn. These chores are always performed at night, for the brownie is careful not to be observed.

Although brownies are usually greatly appreciated for their diligence and industry, they abhor any acknowledgment from humans. The reason for this has been the subject of debate for centuries. One guess is that they are an outlawed clan of spirits who got caught on the losing side in the great war of heaven. They happen to be fascinated by humankind and all our doings, which is why they like to live among us and imitate us. They are very nervous around us, however.

Dealing with brownies

Always take great care not to acknowledge a brownie's presence. Any open display of gratitude, particularly the ostentatious leaving of gifts such as clothing, is likely to result in the brownie disappearing in a huff, never to return. While it is customary to leave food for them at night—preferably milk and cookies—it is best to allow the brownie to think that it has been carelessly left out.

It is also important that you never talk openly about brownies, for they are sharp-eared and suspicious. Above all, never criticize a brownie's work, for this will cause a terrible tantrum and the brownie will stop work. A way around this is to bear in mind that brownies cannot read.

faery helpers

Domovoi

Domovoi are house spirits among the Slavonic people of eastern Europe. They can assume different forms but usually appear as hairy, gray-bearded little men. Domovoi have much in common with the brownies and hobgoblins of western Europe.

In Slavonic tradition there are tales of rebellious spirits who were cast out of heaven and sent down to earth. Those that fell on people's houses became domesticated and useful, those that fell on outbuildings and fields made good guardians and workers but were less tame, and those that fell in wild places were vicious and dangerous. Domovoi are the first kind of spirit.

The hearth bug

Whenever a Slavonic tribal group moved to a new settlement, they were accompanied by their ancestral spirits. Once they had begun to farm their new land and had constructed permanent dwellings, the domovoi moved in, attaching themselves to family units with whom they remained for generations. What they love most about living with people is the warmth of the hearth, for in common with most faeries, they cannot make fire themselves. In traditional Russian houses, the hearth shares a central chimney with the oven. It is there that food is left for the domovoi at night. This keeps them sweet and well-disposed. A domovoi often has a wife, known as a domania or domovikha, who lives under the floorboards or in the cellar.

Guardian and fortune teller

Although the domovoi are useful workers, their most important function is as guardians, defending the house from evil spirits and intruders. Fear of the domovoi was once a sufficient threat to make burglary a rare crime. Domovoi also provide omens of future problems or disasters. This can be as immediate as pulling someone's hair to warn of an impending accident such as a trip or fall, or giving someone a cold, clammy touch to warn of bad luck at some point in the future. A soft, furry touch is a good sign.

Like brownies, a domovoi has quirks. He does not like to be spoken about directly, so people refer to him as himself, grandpa, or chelovka (which means fellow). If angered, he may go as far as burning down the house. He tends to become very attached to his house, however, and when a family moves to a new home, they should place some food near the oven to make sure the domovoi follows.

faery helpers

Wee Willie Winkie

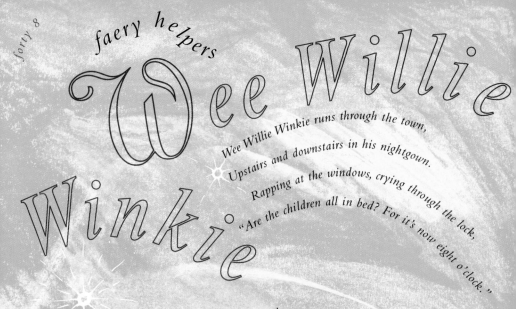

Wee Willie Winkie runs through the town,
Upstairs and downstairs in his nightgown.
Rapping at the windows, crying through the lock,
"Are the children all in bed? For it's now eight o'clock."

Wee Willie Winkie is the most familiar bedtime spirit in English-speaking lands and is famous the world over. He is one of the multitude of nursery spirits created by adults to cajole children into obedience. This is not to say that he does not really exist, of course. He is alive in the active imaginations of millions of children, past and present. It is quite possible that some children impress the personality of Wee Willie Winkie onto their own guardian angels, who can then influence them under this guise.

Bedtime spirits

Like guardian angels, bedtime spirits such as Wee Wilhe and the Sandman (or Dustman), Ole Luke Oie in Scandinavia, and Dormette in France act as protectors of children. They ensure peaceful sleep and inspire sweet dreams, keeping night terrors away. The Sandman sprinkles magic dream-sand in the eyes of drowsy children, while Ole Luke Oie and Wee Willie Winkie take them by the hand and lead them to the wonderful dreamland of Nod.

A helping hand

Such nursery spirits are of invaluable assistance to parents and can even be used as allies to help control bedwetting and sleep walking. Children can be gently and cheerfully encouraged to ask Wee Willie Winkie to wake them if their bladder gets too full or if they get out of bed.

In times of great stress, after upsetting events or perhaps when sleeping in strange beds, gentle sleep spirits can distract children from thoughts that may inspire nightmares or insomnia. Wee Willie Winkie is a particular favorite because he is childlike, funny, just a little bit naughty, and full of the sense of adventure and lively fantasy with which children can easily identify.

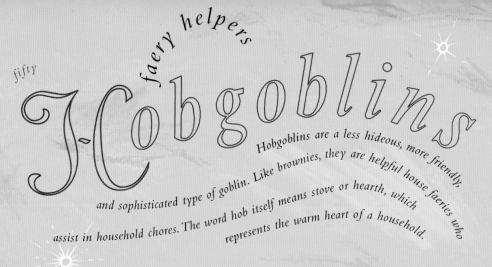

faery helpers

Hobgoblins

Hobgoblins are a less hideous, more friendly, and sophisticated type of goblin. Like brownies, they are helpful house faeries who assist in household chores. The word hob itself means stove or hearth, which represents the warm heart of a household.

Hobgoblins were originally goblins, those malicious sprites who took to inhabiting human dwellings in order to persecute us. However, hobgoblins became more interested in imitating our activities than disrupting them, and came to be very useful additions to the household. They can put their hand to almost any task if the need is urgent, but they tend to specialize in churning milk to make butter or threshing and grinding corn to make flour.

Night workers

Hobgoblins were originally subterranean earth spirits, and as a result they cannot bear the light of day and are active only at night. They love the warmth of kitchen ranges, which is one of the reasons they were drawn to inhabit human dwellings, being unable—as are most faery folk—to work with fire themselves. The replacement of constantly burning ranges with gas and electric ovens in most modern households has contributed to the decline in hobgoblins, who were once quite common.

Less tricksy than brownies

Despite their domestication and their generally helpful attitude, hobgoblins retain some of their goblin mischievousness. They love to play pranks and practical jokes, particularly on lazy, drunken, or bad-tempered people. However, they are never vicious, unless they feel they have been insulted. Indeed, their tricks often offer us the opportunity to recognize our own faults.

Dealing with hobgoblins

Hobgoblins are quite self-confident and relaxed. Unlike brownies, they have no embarrassment about living among us and are therefore much less prickly. They do not mind having their presence acknowledged or being talked about, but they cannot abide criticism. If you should be so fortunate as to have a hobgoblin living in your house, take care not to offend it or it may revert to goblin type and start wreaking havoc. Take care to feed it nightly with bread soaked in milk. Do not think that just because the bread has not been eaten that it has not been touched. Like all faery folk, hobgoblins draw the vital sustenance out of food while leaving the bulk.

Hinzelmann

Hinzelmann is Germany's most well-known house spirit. His story, as recorded by the Grimm brothers, is one of the best-documented cases of a genuine house spirit, fascinating for its wealth of detail and insights into the nature of such spirits.

In 1584 the servants of the old castle of Hudemühlen (now ruined), near Hanover, noticed strange knockings and other noises. Then, to their horror, an invisible spirit began conversing with them. The spirit started addressing the master of the house and was soon a regular presence at mealtimes, discoursing with all present. He gave his name as Hinzelmann and claimed to have come from the Bohemian mountains, where he had fallen out with his fellows.

Willing helper and playful trickster

Gradually the people of the castle became used to Hinzelmann, and as a result, he became increasingly intimate and friendly, laughing, jesting, and singing in a sweet, youthful voice. He loved the company of young people, particularly females. When taunted, however, he could become angry and vindictive, pulling beards and upsetting chairs. Unable to get rid of his new guest, the castle owner decided to move. However, Hinzelmann accompanied him in the form of a white feather and persuaded him to return, promising only goodwill.

Once back, the spirit became most obliging and industrious, helping with all manner of tasks. The cook was particularly fond of him. At his request, a room was set up for him with a table, bed, and a little armchair he made himself. He required feeding with bread soaked in milk, but although the food appeared to be eaten, it was later found in corners or under furniture. Hinzelmann was fond of playing tricks, but they were seldom malicious, although he delighted in bringing the servants to blows when drunk. Lazy servants were often punished and he would regularly chastise people for their faults.

Three parting gifts

Hinzelmann's attachment to the master's two sisters was such that he regularly scared off their suitors, ensuring that they never married. He remained invisible to all but children and the fool Claus, to whom he appeared as a beautiful, golden-haired boy. After four years in the castle, he announced that he was leaving and gave the master three gifts to remember him by: a little plaited cross, a straw hat, and a leather glove, all beautifully made. The hat came into the possession of Emperor Ferdinand II; the other two gifts are lost. Hinzelmann was never heard of again.

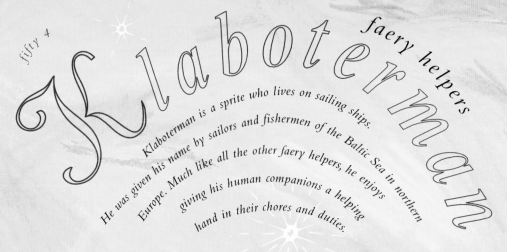

Klaboterman

Klaboterman is a sprite who lives on sailing ships. He was given his name by sailors and fishermen of the Baltic Sea in northern Europe. Much like all the other faery helpers, he enjoys giving his human companions a helping hand in their chores and duties.

Klaboterman is a merry and industrious creature who loves ships and is an expert in all aspects of sailing and ship maintenance. He can hoist and reef sails, stow all manner of cargo in the holds, haul anchor, and scrub decks. Such usefulness makes him a valuable asset and any ship that has him on board may be considered well-blessed.

An indispensable asset

Klaboterman is most indispensable when a ship is in difficulties during storms, and many a sailor may have been lost overboard had he not been saved by him. Lazy sailors who do not pull their weight are not so fond of their invisible companion, however. When he catches them idling, he pinches them, trips them, or plays other pranks to keep them on their toes.

Apart from keeping things shipshape, Klaboterman also helps sustain morale on board. He is very musical and will often get a singsong going by starting to sing a favorite sea shanty that the rest of the sailors then take up. Some shanties have actually been attributed to him.

Omens and ghost ships

In spite of all Klaboterman's positive qualities, it is considered unlucky actually to see him, for he only ever becomes visible to those who are doomed to die. This, of course, makes some sailors fearful of him, and they consider him a bad omen. He therefore figures in stories of ghost ships, those eerie vessels manned by drowned sailors that resurface from their watery graves to haunt the dreams of fishermen and seamen.

However, Klaboterman is undeserving of such morbid associations. After all, he cannot be expected to rescue every sailor washed overboard or felled by a swinging yardarm. Like all spirits, Klaboterman cannot interfere with people's destinies. More positive seafolk consider it good luck to carve a likeness of Klaboterman dressed in yellow clothes with a woolen sailor's cap and a tobacco pipe, which they keep in a safe and honored place or securely attached to the mast.

Ekkekko

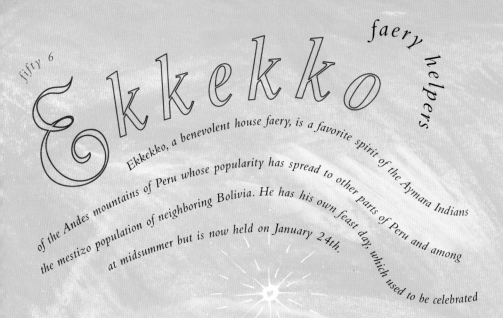

Ekkekko, a benevolent house faery, is a favorite spirit of the Aymara Indians of the Andes mountains of Peru whose popularity has spread to other parts of Peru and among the mestizo population of neighboring Bolivia. He has his own feast day, which used to be celebrated at midsummer but is now held on January 24th.

The indigenous peoples of South America have a worldview that is permeated by spirits. The whole of creation is animated by conscious spiritual intelligences, which they believe need to be acknowledged and appreciated in order to live in harmony with the natural world.

Foes or allies

Most Amazonian and Andean spirits can assume a human form, being distinguished by their behavior, their physiognomy, or strange deformities. Many are horrific, hairy, or skeletal, and hostile toward humans. Some assume the frightening and aggressive aspects of certain wild animals, such as snakes, eagles, and jaguars. Others are friendly and enjoy human company. If propitiated in the right way, they can become allies, assisting in the domain where they have influence, be it hunting, fishing, or some other aspect of life.

Bringer of prosperity and fertility

Ekkekko (also spelled Ekako, Ekeko, or Eq'eq'o) usually takes the form of a fat little man bearing tools and household utensils, which also adorn his clothes. He uses these items to perform all manner of household chores, such as cleaning, grinding corn, mending things, and washing clothes and dishes. He shows none of the trickiness or touchiness common among his European counterparts, such as hobgoblins and brownies. As long as he is treated with respect and consideration, Ekkekko can bring good fortune and prosperity to a household. Ekkekko is also a fertility spirit who can inspire cordial and amorous relations between husbands and wives, and bless a family with healthy children.

La Befana

La Befana is the beloved Christmas faery of Italy who, like Santa Claus, fills children's stockings with candy. She comes not on Christmas Eve, however, but on Twelfth Night, the night of January 5th, the eve of the feast of the Epiphany.

The Epiphany commemorates the joy and wonder of the three Wise Men when beholding the infant Jesus in Bethlehem. La Befana is named after the Italian *epifania*, because of her legendary involvement in this story.

The legend of La Befana

La Befana was an old widow living in a hut outside Bethlehem when the three Wise Men stopped to ask for refreshment. They told her of their mission to follow the bright new star until they found the newborn king. The old crone was invited to join them, but she decided that she was too tired and too busy. Some time after they had departed, she had an epiphany herself, a vision of the glorious child. Full of love, she gathered up some gifts and hurried after the men. She never found them, nor the Christ child, but ever since she has loved all children and been loved by them for her kindness. She continues to go from house to house leaving gifts and looking for the Christ child.

Pagan roots

Although specifically linked to the Christ story, La Befana's roots precede Christianity. The crone is a personification of winter, and sacrificial effigies are still burned in some communities to encourage a fertile spring. The burning of witches assumes a sacrificial aspect in this context. La Befana is depicted as a classic witch with a hooked nose and chin, flying on a broomstick with her bag of gifts.

Welcoming meal

Traditionally, La Befana is provided with a welcoming meal of sausage and broccoli and a glass of wine. Children who catch her entering their room cry "Ecco La Befana!" ("Here's La Befana!") Parents have used La Befana to control their children, warning them that if they do not behave she will leave them only coal. This is often substituted with black-dyed rock candy as a consolation for initial disappointment. In the 1970s the Italian government tried to nullify Epiphany as a holiday. Never have Italian children shown such solidarity. Epiphany was reinstated and La Befana became more popular than ever.

faery helpers

Spae Wives

Spae wives are a kind of female elf native to Iceland, where they are also known as elf damsels. They are descended from the people who erected the old standing stones and they inhabit the ancient burial sites of long barrows and sacred mounds.

In Scandinavia and other Nordic lands, a spae wife is a seer, a wise woman skilled in the art of divination (the word spae means prophesy or farseeing). Spae wives are highly respected members of society. Also known as volvas, these Viking female shamans act as both priestesses and healers. The fact that in Iceland this term has been applied to a type of faery gives an indication of their special abilities and the reverence in which they are held.

Robes and tools of office

A faery spae wife usually appears as a tiny little woman no bigger than a finger. She may be dressed as a peasant woman, but when summoned in the correct manner and provided with a specially prepared seat, she will wear fine clothes—a blue cloak with bejeweled collar, a black lambskin hood lined with white catskin, calfskin boots, and catskin gloves. She sometimes carries a wooden staff with a jewel-embossed brass knob and wears a belt with a fine skin purse hanging from it containing magical talismans for divination.

The skills of spae craft

Faery spae wives can act as seers, giving advice on how to solve problems, avoid certain situations, and sustain harmonious relationships with all things. They can foretell the future by reading the portents revealed by runes, tea leaves, and all other natural signs. They are also expert at healing and know all the magical correspondences and healing properties of herbs.

Human spae wives learn to develop the intuitional skills of spae craft by paying special attention to omens, personal feelings, and forebodings, particularly before special events, large gatherings, and holy feasts, such as Yule (December 20th–31st) and Ostara (spring equinox). By careful observation of events and consequences, they learn to read the outer and inner signs. Traditionally, the best times for divination are the feasts of Waluburg's Night (May Eve) and Midsummer (summer solstice).

Dwarfs

Dwarfs are one of the most well-known and identifiable faery races. These creatures of the earth are skilled and industrious miners, living beneath the ground and inside mountains. They are also expert metalworkers.

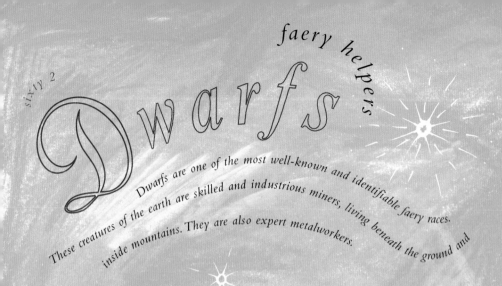

Dwarfs are short, stocky, sometimes rather deformed little people with large heads and long beards. They are very long-lived and hence tend to look rather aged. They wear plain medieval garb with long hoods. Although most dwarfs remain underground, a race of white dwarfs are able to stand daylight and frolic above ground in the form of butterflies during summer, returning to work their mines in winter.

Ancient Germanic lore
Although dwarfs appear all over the world in many different guises, the Teutonic myths of ancient Germany have the richest dwarf lore. According to these legends, dwarfs emerged from the body of the fallen giant Ymir. They were gifted by the gods with an unsurpassed knowledge of minerals and stones of all kinds and an extraordinary talent for working metals, which they are able to endow with magical properties. They repaid

this favor by fashioning the weapons
of the gods, including Thor's hammer,
and the jewelry of the goddesses.

Dwarfs are the natural
proprietors of the precious metals
and gemstones in the earth. The
dwarf Alberich was guardian of the
famous treasure hoard that was won
from him by the hero Siegfried.

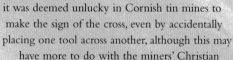

The miners' friends

It was in the shafts and galleries dug into
the sides of mountains that human miners
first encountered dwarfs. Some types of dwarf,
such as the kobolds and knockers, were well-disposed
toward humans, guiding them by the knocking of their picks to
the richest seams of ore. They would warn miners of impending rock falls and explosions. Kobolds
were so drawn to humans that some of them took up residence in their homes, where they became
useful, if mischievous, house spirits. The kobolds also gave their name to the elemental metal cobalt.

Belief in the knockers survives to this day in parts of Europe, and
many so-called superstitions are connected with them. In England,
it was deemed unlucky in Cornish tin mines to
make the sign of the cross, even by accidentally
placing one tool across another, although this may
have more to do with the miners' Christian
fear that the knockers
were of demonic stock.
It was considered foolish
to do anything that
might upset them, for
they could be vengeful.

faery helpers

Menehunes

The volcanic islands of Hawaii are among the most beautiful in the world. The oldest of them is a tropical paradise called Kauai. The native people of the island first arrived on its shores some 1,500 years ago and found the island already populated by a race of tiny magical people called menehunes.

Menehunes have pointed ears, pleasant features, and wear native costume and a little horn around their necks. They usually live below ground in lava tubes, but some inhabit banyan trees and others take up residence in people's houses, as can be deduced from the nocturnal pattering of little feet and the low murmur of their voices.

Refugees from another planet

The Kauaians tell us that the little people of every land all came from a distant planet, which was destroyed. The people of that planet escaped on shooting stars and landed on different parts of Earth, where they are called by different names. When the menehunes landed on Kauai, they planted its wonderful vegetation, transforming it from a barren volcanic desert into a garden isle. When the first humans arrived on the island they were sick, exhausted, and starving. The menehunes took care of them and showed them all over the island, teaching them many wonderful things. It is said that the menehunes disappeared following a great feast that

was prepared in their honor. However, although averse to such ostentatious shows of gratitude, menehunes are grateful for smaller gifts and many islanders still leave food for them.

Shark chasers

Although menehunes are rarely seen these days, their presence is still widely acknowledged throughout the Hawaiian islands. They are believed to be responsible for events that cannot otherwise be explained, such as a structure still standing that should have crumbled years ago. Like so many faeries, they can be mischievous, but they have retained their reputation for being helpful. They are said to protect the islands from tidal waves and shark attacks. They blow their horns to summon seagulls to give them rides and patrol the seashore watching for sharks. If a shark is seen, they call for help and great numbers of them ride out in little boats, beating the waves with their paddles to drive the sharks away.

Clay Mother

Clay mother, or clay woman, is an earth spirit of great cultural significance to the Pueblo peoples of the southwest United States. Clay is the flesh of the earth mother herself, and the working of clay is therefore a sacred act.

To Native Americans the whole of nature is imbued with spirits and intelligences. Even the most inanimate objects, such as stones, have spirits that invest them with their "medicine"—a spiritual significance that informs our understanding. To the Pueblos, it was the earth mother's spirit that first inspired people to take her flesh, or clay, in their hands and fashion vessels and figurines. This gift is greatly treasured and considered as important as the gifts of corn, beans, and salt, which are stored in clay vessels for both practical and ceremonial purposes. When working the clay, Pueblo potters allow the spirit of the clay mother to work through them and express herself in the fashioning of a piece.

Making a clay mother figurine

Although store-bought clay will do, it is preferable to find a natural source because this will help you to connect with the clay mother more intimately. In many areas clay lies beneath the topsoil or in the banks of rivers and streams. If you cannot find any, ask a local geology teacher where to look. Before digging your fingers into it, say a prayer to the clay mother, asking her permission to take of her flesh to make an object that will honor her. Only take the amount that you need.

Mix the clay with water until it is loose enough to work through a sieve. This will remove small stones and other debris. Let it stand in a dry place until it has firmed a little bit and then start kneading it in your hands. Let the clay mother work through you so that she herself is the artist. When you are happy with the result, allow the figurine to dry for a while, then smooth its surface with your fingers. Alternately, paint it with a liquid mixture of clay and water colored with natural pigment. Bake it in the oven, and if all has gone well, you will have your own embodiment of the clay mother to treasure.

Strömkarl

Like all his fellow water spirits, Strömkarl loves music and song. He possesses a magical talent for teaching music, and if you strike the right bargain with him, he will help you play like a maestro.

Strömkarl is Swedish for river man, and this spirit loves fast, rushing water. He therefore chooses to live by waterfalls, weirs, and water mills, and it is at such places that he may be found, playing enchanting melodies. Water spirits such as pixies, sirens, and mermaids all enchant and entice men with their beautiful melodies, while Nicker's singing can be fatally attractive to women. Strömkarl, however, is less perilous to humans.

The spirit of dance

Strömkarl plays a stringed instrument similar to a fiddle or violin, which produces the most fluid and irresistible tones, like the sound of swiftly flowing water. His melody has eleven variations. Ten of these he plays regularly, and their joyful strains may be heard and danced to by all. There is an eleventh variation, however, that he plays at night. The sound of the tune is so thrilling and intoxicating that it possesses all who hear it. Everyone within earshot, be they young, old, sick, lame, or even swaddling babies, feels the music coursing through their bodies like an unstoppable flood, forcing them to give themselves up to rapturous dance. In fact, any object that is not bolted or strapped to the ground, even heavy tools and tables, is unable to resist dancing like a dervish.

Striking a bargain with Strömkarl

Some musicians are rumored to have sold their soul to the devil in return for their talent. Strömkarl, too, can invest people with musical prowess, but the bargain he strikes is not so drastic. The requirements, however, are specific. Musicians must approach a north-flowing waterfall on a Thursday evening. They should offer a black lamb or a young white billy goat as a sacrifice to Strömkarl. Averting their eyes, they should thrust the sacrificial beast into the cataract with their right hand. Strömkarl will seize the sacrifice and shake the musician's hand until blood starts running from the fingertips. If all proceeds correctly, the musician will be able to make the trees dance and the waterfall stand still.

CHAPTER THREE

Tricksters & Seducers

Faeries have a reputation for playing tricks on humans, and we can hardly blame them. To their keen senses, we must seem clumsy and foolish most of the time. Their ability to act upon our plane while remaining invisible or shape-shifting provides them with endless opportunities to tease and mislead us. Some of these tricksters are not malevolent and can make us more self-aware and alert. Others, however, are jealous and vindictive.

Puck

The biggest star in the faery constellation, certainly in English-speaking lands, is Puck. He owes much of his international fame to Shakespeare, who immortalized him in A Midsummer Night's Dream, but he was already well known in the faery kingdom centuries before then.

Puck is a trickster spirit, a merry prankster—mischievous, even vicious, but never evil. His original incarnation was as Bucca, a nature spirit who could control the weather. Bucca is Old English for he-goat, and Puck is often seen with goat's legs and horns, like a faun.

From Bucca are derived the names for various sprites, including buckie, pookie, bogie, bug-a-boo, and bogeyman. However, Puck is not a class of sprite but a very specific individual. He is a shape-shifter who can appear in any guise, and this ability helps him to perform all manner of pranks and trickery.

Maker of mischief

Puck's mischief making is never randomly malicious. He likes to amuse himself at the expense of clumsy, unaware humans, but his teasing often helps us to see through our own foolishness. In this way, he can be a useful ally and guide, particularly if we can learn to laugh at ourselves.

However, woe betide those who transgress natural law, for they make themselves a target for Puck's wrath.

In this sense, he is a spiritual vigilante, punishing those who commit moral crimes that human laws let pass.

Robin Goodfellow

For all his teasing, Puck loves to interact with humans—his alter ego and domestic equivalent is Robin Goodfellow, the house sprite. Robin invites himself into our world out of curiosity and affection, becoming a mirror for human nature.

Befriending Puck

Puck's signature is everywhere in nature, from the friendly robin redbreast to the plants herb Robert and little Robin. Bruise the leaves with your fingers and rub some of the juice behind your ears to win Puck's regard; he may give you insights into the way things really work in the natural world. You should also try being less self-important and develop your sense of fun.

Leprechauns

tricksters

Leprechauns are the famous faery pranksters of Irish folklore. Halfway between a dwarf and an elf, they appear as little, sharp-faced old men with long, gray beards. They delight in misleading and teasing people, particularly those who need to be taught a lesson.

The traditional costume of the leprechaun is a silver-buttoned red jacket, brown britches, buckled shoes, and a red cap. However, this has largely been replaced in the popular imagination by their alternative all-green attire, owing to modern cultural interpretations in movies and books.

Shoemakers and treasure hoarders

Leprechauns are shoemakers and, therefore, take great pride in their own shoes, which are usually black and highly polished with shiny silver buckles. They are solitary figures and are always seen alone, usually sitting beneath a foxglove making a shoe. They live in hollows inside the earth, either in caves or among the roots of ancient trees.

They have a reputation for being treasure hoarders, but the fact is that they have no great use for it themselves. However, they know how greedy we are when it comes to gold and silver and precious stones, and this gives them an opportunity to indulge in their favorite pastime—playing tricks on us. Many of the stories about leprechauns involve gullible humans being taken for a ride in the hope of finding fabulous treasure troves.

Finding a leprechaun's treasure

It is said that if you hear the tapping of a leprechaun's cobbling hammer, and manage to creep up on him unawares, he must answer your questions truthfully as long as you have him fixed in your sight and must lead you to treasure if you so desire. Take your eyes off him even for a second, however, and he will disappear, leaving you lost—as indeed you will be even if you get to the treasure.

The only way to find the treasure without getting lost is to admire his shoes. This may put him off his guard, giving you the opportunity to seize him. In this way you can get him to lead you to the treasure while carefully marking your way. However, such a plan is not to be advised. Even if you are successful, the vengeful little imp is likely to bide his time until an opportunity arises to get his own back.

Gremlins

tricksters

Gremlins are mischievous critters that cause electrical appliances and electronic machinery to malfunction. First identified in the 1920s by British airforcemen, they became famous during World War II for their relentless sabotage of aircraft.

In the 1920s a series of baffling mechanical mishaps at a British airforce base on the northwest frontier in India left mechanics and crew struggling for an explanation. A combination of Grimm's faery tales, the only book in the officers' mess, and Fremlin's beer inspired the name of the culprit.

Media stars

During World War II, pilots claimed to have seen gremlins riding on their wings, drilling holes in fuselage, ripping wires out of engines, and suddenly appearing on the windscreen to frighten them. Subspecies emerged, such as spandules, who were said to ice up wings and flatten propellers. Articles appeared in numerous journals, including the *New York Times Magazine* and the *London Observer*.

Children's author Roald Dahl started a cartoon strip, depicting them as brown-skinned little imps with red noses like tomatoes. He wrote his first book, *The Gremlins*, in 1943 in association with Walt Disney, but the projected animated feature was not made because it was finally deemed to be in bad taste to make gremlins appear cute at a time when thousands of airmen lived in daily fear of them.

The gremlins have landed

After the war the gremlins descended from the skies, no doubt fascinated by the proliferation of new technologies down on land and sea. Now we all know them to be just as likely to cause a computer to crash as an aircraft. However, are they just a convenient excuse for poor workmanship or do they really exist? Well, perhaps gremlins are a particularly curious and intelligent kind of sylph, who are both fascinated and irritated to find these noisy new neighbors flying through their skies. They may have become so intrigued by the workings of machines that they transferred their attention entirely to that domain.

They also have a Puckish quality to them, as avouched by airmen who remarked that gremlins tended to plague careless and slovenly people. On occasion, gremlins are even believed to have saved lives, interceding when disaster seemed inevitable. People who give their cars names have been shown to suffer fewer problems. Perhaps the resident gremlin thinks that it is he who is being respected, and is therefore benignly disposed.

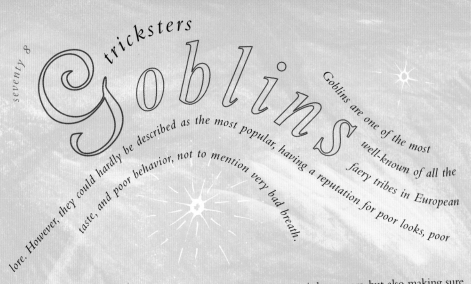

tricksters
Goblins

Goblins are one of the most well-known of all the faery tribes in European lore. However, they could hardly be described as the most popular, having a reputation for poor looks, poor taste, and poor behavior, not to mention very bad breath.

Goblins were originally earth elementals like gnomes, who lived inside the earth, as indeed many still do (this is why they hate light and only operate at night). When humans started mining for metals and minerals, they did their best to disrupt such labors, and as we destroyed their homes, they started following us into ours and taking their revenge at every opportunity.

A bad influence on children

Being short and ugly to the point of hideousness, malicious and spiteful most of the time, and generally a downright nuisance, goblins have very few redeeming features. It is sometimes said in their favor that they like children, even bringing them gifts when they are well-behaved, but this is just a typical example of adults interfering with the facts in order to encourage children to behave. The fact is that while they tend to leave good children alone, goblins are a very bad influence on naughty children, encouraging them to misbehave.

Although children may delight in their wicked sense of humor, goblins do not make loyal allies, not only allowing their human playmates to take all the blame for their misdemeanors, but also making sure that adults get so angry that they mete out severe punishments. Goblins just love to see adults lose their temper. Nothing delights them more than seeing clumsy humans trip over something they have put in their way.

Getting rid of a goblin

If you should suffer the misfortune of having a goblin in your house, there is little you can do about it. However, if you refuse to let it rile you and remain sweet-tempered at all times, it may eventually get bored and look for more exciting entertainment elsewhere. A traditional way of getting rid of a goblin is to cover the floors with flax seed. Apparently, the goblin feels obliged to pick it all up by hand. If there is so much that he cannot finish the task by dawn, he will have no time to cause mischief and will soon move elsewhere.

The Bogeyman

"You had better do what you are told or the bogeyman will come and get you!" This familiar refrain has been used for centuries to frighten children into behaving themselves, but what is the reality of this ghostly being?

The bogeyman, or boogieman, has become a familiar, if somewhat vague, fear form, a lurking monster endowed with varying characteristics. All cultures seem to have their equivalent of the bogeyman.

Eater of souls

The word bogeyman is derived from the same root as bug, bogie, bogle, boggart, bug-a-boo, bug-bear, and bogan, all of which are frightening spirits in British folklore, though with varying attributes. Bogles, for example, are vicious, vengeful sprites, but they only harm those who deserve punishment. This is a familiar notion. Many trickster spirits reserve their mischievous or spiteful pranks for those who need to be taught a lesson. The bogeyman, however, tends to be a less discerning creature.

The bogeyman is amorphous, having neither form nor personality. He is without intelligence or motive. He is a void, an abyss of nonbeing. He may be seen through a knot hole in the wall as a blank spot, a faint shadow, but he is, in reality, no-thing, non-spirit. He is not evil in the sense of wishing to harm or pervert. Indeed, he is no more wicked than a bottomless pit, but he is as perilous to come close to. He is a symbol of death conjured by a guilty conscience. To the natives of Central and South America, he is the jaguar, the eater of souls.

Fear of annihilation

The powerful idea behind the bogeyman is the warning that wrongdoing may cost us our souls. Of all Earth's creatures, humans alone are given the gift of knowing right from wrong. We have the opportunity to attain great things, but, should we abuse life, we may forfeit our own. What makes the bogeyman so frightening is the fear that we project onto the idea of annihilation. This can prove a powerful incentive not to do wrong, but it is not so much the breaking of conventional, social laws we should fear, but rather the breaking of natural law. The bogeyman loses his power when we realize that love and consideration are better incentives to developing a conscience than fear. When we are on the side of life, we need have no fear of death.

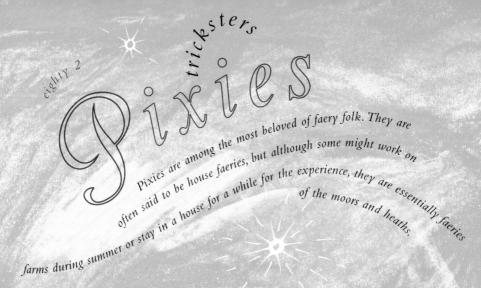

Pixies

tricksters

Pixies are among the most beloved of faery folk. They are often said to be house faeries, but although some might work on farms during summer or stay in a house for a while for the experience, they are essentially faeries of the moors and heaths.

Pixies are not dissimilar in appearance to Disney's Peter Pan, having elfish faces, though somewhat rounder, with pointed ears and upturned noses. They always wear green and favor little pointed caps—that is, when they appear in human form, for they are capable of assuming lots of different shapes.

Zest for life

Pixies belong to that genus of beings who were deemed not good enough for heaven, nor bad enough for hell, and doomed to wander the earth forever, which sounds like most of us. This is most likely the truth of it, rather than later Christian superstition that reckoned them to be the souls of unbaptized infants. Either way, pixies certainly have a great zest for life and are childlike by nature. They are clever and quite cunning, with a fair degree of self-awareness.

Pixy-led to a world of fancies

Pixies tend to be nocturnal and it is at night that you are most likely to find yourself being pixy-led— that is, led astray by the pixies. This gives them great delight, and many is the tale of lonely travelers on the moors who find themselves led into a bog or around and around in circles. Pixies also have a great fondness for horse racing. They mount moorland ponies or steal a farmer's horse and race them frantically around gallitraps, little circles of mushrooms also known as faery rings.

The best chance of seeing pixies is on a moor during the fall, when they will even frolic about during daytime. If spotted, they usually turn themselves into mushrooms with caps the same shape as their own. Foolhardy people who eat these mushrooms find that they have ingested a pickle of pixies, who then proceed to make them wild with fancies and so helpless with laughter that they roll upon the ground. Should the mushroom eaters be able to master themselves, the pixies might lead them on a great adventure and show them some of their secret places.

seducers

The Snow Queen

The Snow Queen is the arch-seductress of faeryland who casts her icy glamor on young men in an attempt to steal their souls. Traditionally she lives in a palace of ice in a snowbound realm of perpetual winter, peopled by other cold-blooded creatures that share her hatred of humanity, light, and warmth.

The Snow Queen is an archetypal example of a spirit in revolt against the light, a fallen angel who refuses to serve god or man. She is, in fact, a genderless vampiric spirit who disguises herself as an impossibly beautiful woman in order to lure her victims. Once enchanted, they become listless and enfeebled, unable to break away until, if they are lucky, the spell is broken, usually by the selfless love of a real woman.

Soul stealer

Although the Snow Queen is immortal, she craves one thing that will add to her power, something humans have but spirits lack—a soul. She preys on humanity not only for sustenance but also out of jealous hatred. She is further embittered by the fact that, while she can trap souls and drain them of energy, she cannot really appropriate them—she remains soulless herself. Another way in which she steals energy is by insinuating herself into the minds of men as the perfect, unattainable woman, making them unable to fall in love with another.

Protecting yourself from the Snow Queen

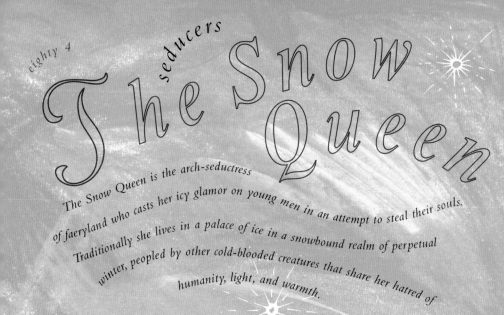

Two herbs can be used to thwart the Snow Queen. The first is mugwort, which you should wear as a protective amulet, and the other is St.-John's-wort, whose solar energy can thaw hearts frozen by her icy grip. Both these herbs are sacred to St. John, protector against the forces of darkness, whose saint's day is June 24th. This is midsummer day in the northern hemisphere, when the power of the sun is at its height.

Nicker

Nicker is a dangerous water faery of Norse tradition, who is known by similar names throughout the northernmost lands of Europe. He appears in various guises, ranging from a handsome youth to a centaur or white horse with hooves facing backward.

Nicker can be seen standing by the edge of rivers, streams, lakes, or seas. He makes beautiful, enchanting music, either singing or playing an instrument. He is, therefore, a male siren of sorts, although his playing and singing are not necessarily intended to lure people to their doom. He is said to be harmless if left alone, but disaster can ensue if he is approached. Nicker is attracted to human women, who easily fall captive to his charms. He is said to be a wonderful, passionate, and caring lover, but can turn murderous when scorned.

Fear of water

If Nicker is mounted when in the form of a horse, he plunges into the water and drowns his rider. In this respect he closely resembles the kelpie of Scottish legend, a horrifying water demon with no redeeming features whatsoever. Both Nicker and the kelpie are composite creatures—in essence, powerful water spirits onto whom archetypal psychological anxieties have been projected. Bodies of water were generally feared in past times, not just

because most people could not swim but also because deep water was believed to conceal monsters and demons. Water symbolizes the unconscious, the primordial, and submersion in water represents loss of identity and death. Water is also symbolic of the faery realm itself, with all its attractions and dangers.

White horses

An interesting aspect of both kelpie and Nicker folklore is their identification with horses, particularly white horses in Nicker's case. Horses are powerfully symbolic of intense desires and instincts, sexuality, magic, water, and death. To dream of a white horse was considered an omen of death—white horses are the foam-flecked waves on a rolling sea; the stallion is powerful, irresistible sexuality. Nicker is, therefore, a cautionary figure—to give in to the seductiveness of longing and desire for the wild is to make yourself vulnerable to powerful forces that might drag you into the depths, where you could lose yourself entirely, never to return.

Sirens

seducers

Sirens are malicious sea nymphs who sometimes appear as half woman, half bird and sometimes as a woman. They perch on rocks and sing and play music of beguiling sweetness in order to attract passing ships. Ships that draw too near are wrecked on the rocks, and the sirens then devour any unfortunate sailors.

Sirens are to be found in the Mediterranean Sea, where their activities are recorded in Greek mythology. They are said to be the daughters of Phorcys, one of the ancient sea gods, or of Melpomene, the muse of tragedy, and the river god Achelous. All sirens have incredibly beautiful voices, and some of them also play instruments such as flutes and lyres.

Thwarted by heroes

During his epic voyage home from Troy, Odysseus's ship was approaching an island inhabited by sirens. Odysseus was determined to hear their legendary music, but knowing their murderous reputation, he took the wise precautions suggested by the sorceress Circe. He had his men lash him to the mast and ordered them not to untie him, no matter how much he pleaded. He then instructed them to put beeswax in their ears so that they would not hear the sirens. As the ship passed by the island, Odysseus was captivated by their music. Crazy with desire to draw nearer to them, he screamed and raved at his men to untie him, but deaf to his entreaties, they ignored him and rowed on until the sirens were safely out of earshot.

During their epic quest, Jason and the Argonauts also sailed close to a siren island. One of the Argonauts was Orpheus, who sang so beautifully that his companions were immune to the sirens' voices and the *Argo* sailed safely by. The sirens are said to have been so enraged that they threw themselves into the sea and drowned.

The legend of Lorelei

Sirens inspired the legend of Lorelei, a spirit who inhabited the Lorelei rock on the river Rhine in Germany. She, too, lured sailors to their deaths with her beautiful singing, and her rock has become a tourist attraction. Her story is, in fact, told in a novel published in 1800. All sirens, whether real or imaginary, represent the temptation of desire and warn that all that glitters is not gold, and what sounds sweet and true may conceal a vicious motive.

Morgan le Fay

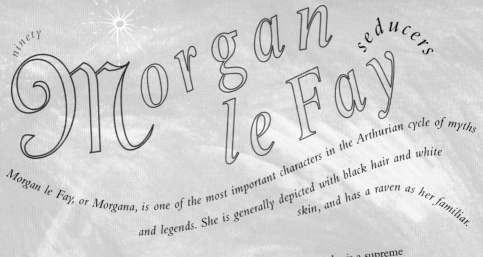

Morgan le Fay, or Morgana, is one of the most important characters in the Arthurian cycle of myths and legends. She is generally depicted with black hair and white skin, and has a raven as her familiar.

Stories of Morgan le Fay portray her in many guises: evil sorceress, beautiful seductress, wise healer, queen, priestess, mother, wife, crone. The origins of her name also display her diverse characteristics—it means mermaid ("morgen" in Brittany, France), murderous siren ("fata morgana" in Italy), faery ("fay" means faery), shape-shifting war goddess (Morrigan), and even the Celtic mother goddess (Modron) herself.

Arthurian legend

In medieval Arthurian romances Morgan le Fay is depicted as both Arthur's half-sister and his principal adversary, a beautiful, scheming enchantress who uses her cunning to imprison Merlin the wizard, undermine the round table, and reduce Arthur's kingdom to ruin. She even incestuously bears him a son, the evil Mordred, who eventually kills Arthur in battle. However, she also appears as one of the priestesses who bear Arthur's body to the faery isle of Avalon, redeeming them both. What is revealed in the quest for the real

Morgan le Fay is that she is a supreme feminine archetype. This is why she is pitched in conflict with Arthur, who in turn represents a supreme male archetype. It is through the feminine that man attains wisdom. She initiates the tasks and ordeals through which Arthur and his knights must triumph in the quest for true kingship and nobility.

The holy grail

This search for wisdom finds its highest expression in the quest for the holy grail. Morgana traps Merlin in a crystal prison so that the knights of the round table have no recourse to magic. The grail must be found through courage and nobility alone. The grail itself exists in a realm between our material world and the feminine faery world of spirit.

Morgana confronts Arthur, because she is his opposing partner in the duality of man and woman. The reconciliation of opposites is the purpose of the love story that is life. Morgan le Fay is therefore the very essence of the female as guide to the faery realm.

Lamia

Lamia is a frightful, ghoulish creature, a shape-shifting vampire who can assume the form of a beautiful woman. More frequently, however, she appears with a woman's head and a snake's scaly body, and one of her earliest portraits depicts her as a four-footed monster with paws in front and hooves behind.

Lamia's story is a sad one. Greek mythology relates that she was once a beautiful maiden beloved of the god Zeus, who fathered many children by her. Sadly, Zeus's jealous wife Hera caused each of these children to die and turned Lamia into a hideous monster so that Zeus would spurn her. The grieving Lamia hid herself in a cave, but the anguish of her loss turned her into a vengeful spirit who started preying on young children, destroying the very things that she most craved. Children would be warned not to cry or Lamia would get them. Her wounded maternal instincts draw her to crying children, who she then kills in repetition of the murder of her own children.

Vampire spirit

Lamia represents a powerful form of fear, and her equivalents can be found in most traditional cultures around the world. She is one of the principal models for the vampires of more recent legend. Her name is derived from lamios, which is the Greek word for throat, the vampire's favorite part of the body.

Demon lover

Lamia is more than just a fear form, however. She is a metaphor for love turned into hate, the inversion of maternal instincts. She also wreaks her revenge on the male sex that spurned her. She becomes a succubus, a demon lover who visits men by night and drains them of vitality.

Despite this, she still craves love and the secure marital state that was denied her. A famous tale is told by Philostratus, a teacher in ancient Greece, of how Lamia caused a young philosopher to fall in love with her, promising years of marital bliss. The great sage Apollonius came to the wedding and realized what she was. He denounced her and she, her house, and all her possessions instantly disappeared.

Lamia's terrible power can only be dissolved by compassion and a deep faith in the consoling, redemptive principle of a caring universe.

Mermaids

seducers

Mermaids are among the most timeless and universal beings of the magical world. With the head and body of a beautiful woman and the tail of a fish, they use their lovely voices to lure sailors to them.

Nowadays mermaids are generally seen as charming, lovable creatures. However, before Hans Christian Andersen's *The Little Mermaid*, a heartbreaking tale of self-sacrificing love, these sea creatures had a far more sinister image.

Seductresses of the deep

Like the fateful sirens of Greek mythology, mermaids were once perceived as dangerous, untrustworthy seductresses, whose motivation was to lure men to a watery grave. This image is a classic example of male projection, involving fear of archetypal, elemental femininity.

The metaphors are obvious: watery depths/female sexuality; drowning/loss of identity. Most heavily emphasized is the powerfully seductive force of attraction, which a man must resist if he is not to be annihilated. Mermaids are also described as carrying a comb and a mirror, suggesting a shallow and calculating vanity.

Healing and reconciliation

There are a few clues in the old legends, however, that suggest a deeper significance. Sometimes mermaids reveal a knowledge of healing herbs that they freely impart to save life, usually that of a wife dying of consumption. Consumption is a disease of the lungs, which might be described as a slow drowning.

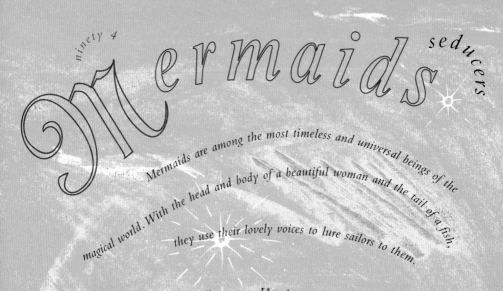

There is clearly a reconciliation necessary. The feminine side of the human character that relates to mermaids should reject vanity for compassion, seeking to rescue rather than to drown. The masculine side that fears mermaids needs to embrace her as a feminine archetype that can guide us into the depths, knowing that she can save us from drowning. In a sense, mermaids connect us to an ancient part of ourselves that evolved in the ocean depths, a part that we have forgotten, a part that we need to embrace.

CHAPTER FOUR

Angelic Faeries

Many of the faery tribes are said to have been among the fallen angels expelled from heaven. Some became wicked little demons, but others continue to seek the divine light and have retained an angelic nature. All of these latter spirits are well-disposed toward humans, believing that we have a special role to play in creation. Some retain a playful tricksiness, but they are all potential allies, willing to act as guides and guardians on the path of light.

The Blue Faery

The blue faery is known to most of us as the angelic guiding spirit in the story of Pinocchio, the wooden puppet who becomes a real boy. Although she appears in many different guises, her color is always blue.

There are few references to the blue faery in the annals of faery folklore, but she is, in fact, a personification of the mother goddess figure. In Catholic cultures she is represented by the Virgin Mary, in Judaism by the Shekinah, and in Mexico by the Lady of Guadalupe, also affectionately known as Guadalupita. To the ancients she was the goddess Isis. All apparitions of these great feminine spirits stem from the same source. They are usually associated with miraculous events or cures and very often feature the color blue. This is the color of the cloak worn by the Virgin Mary, Isis, and the Lady of Guadalupe. Blue represents purity, higher consciousness, and the quality of mercy.

The spirit of compassion

The blue faery, in all her guises, is a compassionate guardian spirit who intercedes on our behalf to deliver us from evil and distress. As in the story of Pinocchio, she can make our most heartfelt dreams become reality if we are true to ourselves. This requires a highly developed conscience and scrupulous personal honesty. Such is the depth of her compassion that, no matter how bad our transgressions, she always responds to humility with comfort and guidance.

Fireflies and little birds

The blue faery is frequently portrayed making a stunning entrance as a dazzling, angelic apparition. However, she does not always make her presence felt in such a dramatic fashion. In cases of spiritual distress she need only appear in the form of a blue firefly or blue bird in order to dispel all terror, anguish, and despair. Such gentle, undramatic apparitions are relatively common.

Béfind

angelic faeries

Béfind is a very special faery in Celtic tradition. She is one of three faeries (the names of the other two are secret) who attend the birth of every child in order to bestow the infant with talents and make predictions about the child's destiny.

We generally call a person's talents "gifts," because they are indeed the gifts of the gods or faeries. It was traditional in Celtic lands to set up a table in the room where the birth was to take place and deck it with dainty cakes for the faeries as a thanksgiving for these gifts. Faeries such as Béfind are probably most familiar to us from the story of Sleeping Beauty, where the good faeries attend the princess's birth to give her their blessings and attempt to protect her from the fateful prediction of the evil faery.

Birth faeries

The story of three birth faeries is not unique to Celtic tradition. The Greeks referred to the three birth spirits as the Moirae, and the Romans called them the Fates. Similarly, the Fatit of Albania derive their name from the Fates of Italy. These destiny spirits arrive shortly after a baby's birth, borne along by the beating of butterflies' wings.

Gypsy birth spirits

In Serbia they revere a single birth spirit called Oosood. She is one of the Veela, a tribe of beautiful nymph-like faeries made famous in the Harry Potter stories. Oosood visits a child on the seventh night after its birth to make her pronouncements about its destiny. She can only be seen by the baby's mother. The gypsies of eastern Europe call their three Fates the Urme. The Urme appear on the third night after the birth and can be seen only by the mother and the midwife.

The Nornir

In Norse lands the Fates are known as the Nornir. These three sisters live at the foot of Yggdrasil, the sacred ash tree that forms the axis of the world. They represent the three aspects of time, as do all Fates. Udur represents the past; Verdandi, the present; and Skuld, the future. They also appear at the birth of children to decide their destiny. They wear long gray veils over their faces and flowing gray robes.

Peris

angelic faeries

Peris are among the most lovely and enchanting of all faery tribes. Like the flower faeries, they are perfectly beautiful miniature versions of ourselves, childlike and graceful with gauzy wings. They live on perfume and nectar and are entirely benign.

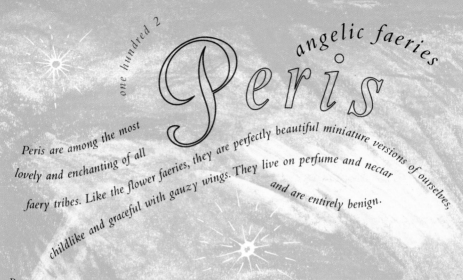

Peris were originally feared as malevolent demons who caused floods and famines and other natural disasters. The ancient Persians believed them to be the offspring of fallen angels who had been expelled from paradise for their vanity, pride, and rebelliousness.

Children of fallen angels

In Islamic tradition, peris are self-conscious spirits of a lower angelic order, who were too busy enjoying themselves to take part in the great war of heaven. For failing to join the angels of light in the struggle against evil, they were expelled from paradise. Although they later repented their selfishness, their supplication under their leader Eblis came too late to allow their readmittance into paradise. Stranded between heaven and hell, and disconsolate at their exile, peris were nevertheless sustained by their sheer zest for life and contented themselves with reveling in nature. They now spend their time assisting the nature devas with joyful exuberance.

Victimized by bullying demons

A peri's life was not always one of constant pleasure, however, for they were plagued by the deevs, a lower class of evil demon who delighted in persecuting them. Deevs saw the peris as feckless, and lacking sufficient self-esteem to join the rebel cause. They would trap peris and lock them in iron cages suspended from treetops. Other peris would then have to risk bringing them nectar to prevent them from fading away, for peris are not necessarily immortal and can be starved to death.

Redemption

The prophet Mohammed was instructed by the archangel Gabriel to preach the word of Islam to the peris and convert them. Since then, peris have been particularly benevolent toward humanity, trusting that our salvation will redeem the whole universe and reopen the gates of paradise to them.

The Angirasah

angelic faeries

The angirasah are a clan of seven immortal beings celebrated in the Vedas, the ancient sacred texts of the Hindu religion in India. These spirits owe their name to their progenitor Angiras, one of the wisest beings in the universe.

It was the angirasah who discovered the fire god Agni residing in dry wood, and found that by rubbing two pieces of wood together the friction generated would produce the sacred fire. They gave this precious gift to humankind and ever since they have presided over ritual fire ceremonies. Hindus traditionally cremate their dead on open fires, and the angirasah feed the purifying flames with their fiery energy to help carry the souls of the dead to the spiritual realms.

Divine consciousness

The angirasah are specifically associated with divine fire, the sacred spark within all things. The idea of fire is inherent in their name, which means "flaming" or "glowing." This is a quality they have in common with the angels of western tradition, who are sometimes referred to as "the flaming ones." Like angels, they act as intermediaries and messengers between the divine realms and humankind. They also protect humans and assist those on the path of consciousness with their great wisdom. Unlike salamanders, the elemental beings whose consciousness is limited to the element fire, the angirasah partake of the divine consciousness of Brahman, the indestructible, absolute consciousness of the universe.

Lighting a purifying fire

Whenever we light a ritual fire for any sacred ceremony, the angirasah are always in attendance. To celebrate this miracle, you can learn to produce fire by simply rubbing two pieces of dry wood together, calling upon the angirasah, the burning powers of the divine spark, to assist you in your endeavor. When the spark catches and springs into flame, feed it lovingly and gratefully, allowing the purifying fire to burn away everything in your being that is not love.

Erotes

angelic faeries

Erotes are the little winged attendants and messengers of the god Eros. In classical Greek art, they are depicted as slender and graceful young men, unlike the chubby prepubescent cherubs who replaced them in Renaissance art.

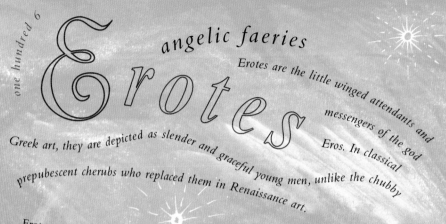

Erotes are invariably depicted naked and often carry a bow and arrows. They appear on many Greek vases riding dolphins, hovering over lovers, and suckling Aphrodite/Venus, the goddess of love.

Eros, god of love and education

Eros is the Greek god of love, called Cupid by the Romans. He is variously said to be the oldest and youngest of the gods. This is because the original act of creation is essentially a sexual act, but one that is eternally repeated in the reproductive processes of nature. He also presides over education, providing another key to his significance, for it is through love and learning that we achieve true understanding. This is why he sends out the erotes, armed with the arrows of desire, for it is through desire that we initiate the experiences that lead us to understanding.

Life is a love story

The erotes are essentially miniature duplicates of Eros. From the erotes' point of view, life is a love story. We are all in a constant love relationship with life itself. Our true happiness and spirituality are defined from one minute to the next by how deeply in love we are with life. The erotes' function is to keep humanity full of love and inspired to forge an ever deeper intimacy with the true nature of existence. The love darts they fire are shots of erotic energy, the most potent expression of life force in the universe.

Guardians and house spirits

There were originally just three erotes, called Himerus, Anteros, and Pothos. However, they must have had their own love affairs, for their numbers grew. There became enough of them to act as guardian angels to the offspring of the unions they inspired, accompanying every child from the cradle to the grave, and then guiding the soul in the afterlife. It seems they became so numerous that they also assumed roles as useful household spirits, for they are sometimes depicted performing domestic chores.

Lauma

angelic faeries

Lauma is a solitary woodland faery in Baltic mythology. She is said to be a beautiful naked woman, with blue eyes and blonde hair, who lives by rocks and pools deep in the woods. She is a protector of the poor and a guardian spirit to orphaned children.

Lauma was originally one of the swan maidens, a lovely sky spirit whose compassion for the suffering of humankind brought her down to dwell on land and involve herself in our fate. She has infinite compassion and understanding for the poor and destitute, and was greatly loved and revered, particularly by women, who honored her with gifts of linen and woven cloth. Lauma is usually encountered by mortals when she is bathing at night or engaged in spinning or weaving by her dwelling.

Spiritual foster mother

Lauma assists women during pregnancy and participates at every birth, ensuring, as far as possible, the welfare of both child and mother. She becomes a spiritual foster mother to those children who lose their mothers or are abandoned. She spins the threads of life, which she then weaves into the cloth of every child's life, determining the story of their lives from birth to death. She often weeps as she weaves, seeing as she does how our destinies will unfold, for although fate unfolds through her, the cloth in a sense weaves itself, dictated by a higher, more mysterious power than Lauma.

Cruel rejection

Perhaps Lauma also weeps at her own fate, for over the years her image gradually changed for the worse. She developed a reputation for vindictiveness, particularly toward men who failed to respect women. Those who suffered at her hands fought back, accusing her of baby snatching, being unable to bear children of her own. She lost her looks as well as her sweetness and was gradually transformed into an evil old hag, with her most vicious detractors even accusing her of killing babies. This cruel and tragic fate is shared by many former gods and goddesses. To re-enchant the world, we need to tell stories of how evil hags are transformed into the eternally beautiful, angelic spirits that they really are. The wheel has turned. The fate of poor Lauma is now in our hands.

Genies

angelic faeries

These engaging spirits are known to the world through the Arabian tales of the Thousand and One Nights, particularly the story of Aladdin. According to Islamic tradition, they were created by Allah from the desert wind and typically appear as dust devils, though they can assume any form they wish.

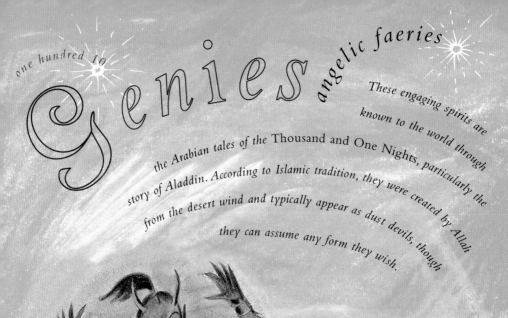

The collective noun for these beings is jinn, with jinnee or genie being the singular form. This is the root of the Latin word genius, meaning spirit, as in guardian spirit or tutelary spirit. Their relationship with humankind is ambivalent, however. They can be extremely malicious toward humans, assuming the form of hideous and terrifying demons or beautiful women who trap men with their charms. When controlled by evil sorcerers, they can harm those toward whom their attention is directed. On the other hand, they can be extremely benevolent, as in the case of Aladdin's lamp genie.

Magic and sorcery

If a sorcerer or magician knows how to control them correctly, genies can be used to perform any manner of task. They can manipulate time and the weather, report on events or conversations from a distance, assist in healing, and provide all kinds of useful information. Fear of the occult and sorcery led to the prohibition of such magical

practices both in Islam and Christendom, with
practitioners being persecuted regardless of their
intentions. Arab alchemists, however, who often
had powerful patrons, were able to sustain a
working relationship with the jinn in the context
of their practical work, with less fear of reproach.
Some of them even knew how to create beings
of limited consciousness called homunculi, as
related in the story of Sinbad.

Guiding genies

In some traditions each one of us is believed
to be assigned both a good and a bad genie,
who remain with us for life, each attempting to
influence our actions for good or ill. The word jinn
can also be used to refer to all spirits that are not
committed to doing good. This does not necessarily
mean they are evil, but simply that their consciousness
may be limited and not attuned to moral considerations.
They are no better or worse than we are. Like us, they can
also evolve their consciousness according to their will.

Tooth Faeries

angelic faeries

Tooth faeries leave money (silver) under children's pillows in exchange for baby teeth, which they use to make stars for the night sky. This motivates children to improve their oral hygiene, because only healthy teeth can be used for this purpose.

The origins of tooth faeries are unclear. In the United States and Britain they certainly date back several hundred years, but there are some indications that they may be of more ancient Viking origin. The exchange of money for a tooth may be connected to the old idea of "an eye for an eye, a tooth for a tooth." It may also have been a way of making sure that teeth were safely collected and not left lying around by children, where they might fall into the hands of malicious people who could use them to perform witchcraft. Fearful people would burn all hair and nail cuttings to stop witches from using them to attack the owner with hexes.

Nursery helper

Nowadays we see tooth faeries as useful nursery spirits, like Wee Willie Winkie. The loss of milk teeth can be distressing and painful for small children, but the promise of a tooth faery, magically exchanging a lost tooth for a coin, can make the discomfort more bearable.

Tooth faeries can also be employed to encourage children to brush their teeth. If tooth faeries start to notice that many of the teeth arriving from Earth are decayed and discolored, they ask Vesta, the wisest of the faeries, to investigate this problem. She finds that the children are eating far too many sweet foods, making their teeth unsuitable as shining stars.

Silver, the faery metal

Silver is the metal of the moon, the ruling planet of the feary realm where tooth faeries live. It is the metal of exchange in magic, medicine, and divination—a gypsy's palm must be "crossed with silver" before she will read your fortune. There are many variations on how to position a tooth for a tooth faery to collect and what to leave in exchange. The tooth is usually placed about twelve "fingersteps" under the child's pillow, which allows the careful parent to replace it without waking the child. Some parents prefer to leave a little silver keepsake in its place rather than a coin, to discourage the child from becoming too materialistic.

CHAPTER FIVE

Rituals & Recipes

The preceeding chapters described many ways in which you can engage with particular faeries. Here, you will discover more about how to deal with faeries in general, including which trees, plants, and foods they prefer. You will also find some crucial tips on how to make faeries visible to you, how to attract them to your home ... and how to evict them if they prove to be more troublesome than you had bargained for.

Seeing Faeries

rituals & recipes

Some people are fortunate enough to be born with "the sight," allowing them to see faeries and experience clairvoyant visions. The rest of us, however, have to try harder to develop these abilities.

Faeries tend to reveal themselves to ordinary mortals only when they want to, but we can improve our chances enormously by doing the following:

• Go to a spot where faeries are likely to be, such as a quiet area where faery trees or flowers grow (see pages 122–125). Woods where bluebells or rings of mushrooms flourish are particularly good locations.

• Choose your time well. The best times are dawn, noon, dusk, and midnight when the moon is full. May and October are particularly good months. Midsummer Eve (June 22nd in the northern hemisphere; December 22nd in the southern hemisphere) is ideal.

• Be sure to have no iron about your person. The only faeries that do not mind it tend to be ones you would not wish to see.

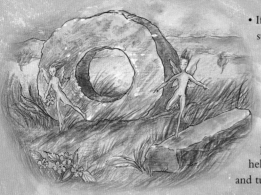

• If you are lucky enough to find a stone with a naturally bored hole in it (known as a holey stone), looking through the hole can improve your chances considerably.

• Try to tune in to the faeries. Hold an idea of them in your mind—not so much an image as a sense of their personality. Just like dowsing, this can help you find their resonating frequency and tune in to their channel.

Faery ointment

A drop of faery ointment smeared on the eyelids can help you to see the little people. Unfortunately, no human has ever discovered the complete recipe, although the following ingredients are known:

> *Four-leaf clover*
> *Hazel flower buds*
> *Elecampane buds*
> *Hollyhock buds*
> *Marigold buds*
> *Thyme buds*

There are a couple of other ingredients, but you will have to guess them. One of them may be fern seed, another vervain buds. There is also the legendary moly, a plant considered by most to be mythical, but who can say for sure. The flower buds should be picked just as they are about open, ideally at full moon. Bruise all of the ingredients together in a mortar, then add them to a small bottle of vegetable oil, ideally hazelnut oil. Leave the oil in a warm, dark spot for a couple of weeks, then filter and bottle it. If you do see a faery, hold it in your gaze; do not even blink or it could disappear.

one hundred 17

Attracting Faeries

The best way to invite faeries to share your home is to act as if they are already there. When you get up in the morning, pause to thank them for their presence and the blessings that they bring.

Once a faery has come to visit your home, wait for a day or two to make sure that it is of the friendly sort. If it is not, turn to pages 120–121 to find out what to do. If you decide that the faery would be a welcome addition to your home, however, here are a few things you can do to encourage it to stay:

- Try to cultivate a sense of wonder, reverence, and fun, as these are moods faeries appreciate.
- Build a faery grotto with stones and crystals, such as quartz and amethyst.
- Faeries are very sensitive creatures, so take care not to offend them by referring to them directly. They especially do not like the word faery, so use the term good folk, gentry, themselves, or any other polite euphemism if you need to talk about them, though it really would be better if you did not.

• House faeries appreciate having food left out for them at night. Bread, milk, and faery flatcakes (see recipe below) are perennial favorites.

• Plant some of their favorite flowers (see pages 122–123). As a special sign of welcome, weave a faery garland from the flowers and hang it on your front door.

• Keep your home reasonably tidy—faeries hate a mess.

Faery food

Faeries love food, particularly dairy products, bread, cakes, and cookies. To make the faery flatcakes below, it is best to use organic and unprocessed ingredients if possible.

3 oz (90 g) porridge oats
3 oz (90 g) mixed seeds
(sesame, poppy, sunflower, or others)
1 oz (30 g) chopped hazelnuts
1 oz (30 g) condensed milk
2 oz (60 g) honey
3 oz (90 g) butter

Melt the honey, milk, and butter in a saucepan. Remove from the heat and stir in the remaining ingredients. Press the mixture firmly into a shallow, well-greased, 8-in (20-cm) square baking pan and place in the oven at 350°F (180°C/gas mark 4) for 30 minutes. Allow to cool, then cut into small squares while still warm.

Do not worry if the food you leave out does not appear to have been eaten. Being only semi-corporeal at most, faeries seldom actually consume the body of the food. Rather, they extract its essence. Faery food should therefore be discarded after a day because it will have little nutritional value left.

rituals & recipes

Discouraging Faeries

Although encountering a faery is usually a wonderful experience, not all faery folk are fun to be with. Luckily, there are some traditional ways to discourage their attentions and to persuade them to leave if they do come to visit.

Should you be unfortunate enough to encounter one of the less friendly little people, here are some things you can do to control the situation:

• Do not accept the first thing a faery offers you or you will be indebted to that faery.

• Be sure to get the last word in any verbal exchange. This will ensure that you are in charge, particularly if you can make your parting words rhyme.

• If you think that faeries are "casting a glamour" over you—that is, making you see things or leading you astray—turn your hat or coat inside out. To prevent it from happening in the first place, carry a four-leaf clover.

• The following plants offer protection from unfriendly faeries: St.-John's-wort; daisies, particularly when worn as a necklace or bracelet; a twig each of oak, ash, and hawthorn tied in a cross with red thread and hung on the front door; an acorn carried in your pocket.

• Faeries hate salt, so sprinkle it around the home to keep them out. Strangely, placing a sock under your bed will also do the trick.

How to "lay" a faery

Many people would be enchanted to have a faery take up residence in their home, but should you have an unacceptably troublesome one, the following rituals will usually encourage them to leave. This is known as "laying" a faery.

First, make a suit of little clothes and leave it out at night. Why this should work is a mystery. Some say it offends the faeries; others say that it makes them so proud they consider themselves too good to associate with humans anymore. If this does not work, sprinkle rice or poppy seeds on the floor. The faery will feel compelled to pick them up and will soon tire of the task and disappear. If the faery proves to be particularly stubborn, try going around the house ringing bells and clapping loudly—they hate the noise. As a last resort, you could risk criticizing them aloud and calling them faeries, but this can have some unpleasant consequences.

Fey Herbs

rituals & recipes

There are many plants associated with faeries. These are known as fey herbs and have special virtues and properties that can connect us with, or protect us from, the little people.

Here is a list of the most well-known.

Bay Attracts benevolent spirits and protects against malicious faeries. Burn the leaves and oil to help open a portal to the faery realm.

Bluebell Bluebell woods are favorite faery haunts. Try sitting in one at noon on a bright, sunny day when the bluebells are in full bloom. You will be able to sense them even if you cannot see them.

Buckthorn Mark out a circle with buckthorn and dance in it under a full moon. If an elf appears, say "Halt and grant my boon!" before it disappears. The elf is then obliged to grant you a wish.

Clover All clovers are sacred to faeries, especially red clover. Four-leaf clovers are a sure sign of faery presence and are a key ingredient of faery ointment (see page 117).

Elecampane Scatter the root on the floor or wear it as an amulet to attract faeries. The flower buds are an ingredient of faery ointment.

Fern If you sit quietly in a silent, fern-covered spot at night, Puck may appear at the stroke of midnight with a gold-filled purse.

Foxglove Also called faery gloves or faery caps, these attract faeries.

Gorse Grow this prickly shrub to keep faeries out.

Heather An indicator plant for the presence of elves and pixies.

Herb Robert Sacred to Puck, as is its smaller cousin, little Robin.

Hollyhock The flower buds are an ingredient of faery ointment.

Lilac Faery folk love the scent of lilac. Lilac wine can produce faery visions.

Marigold The flower buds are an ingredient of faery ointment.

Peony The seeds and roots are traditionally hung around children's necks to guard them against harmful or mischievous faeries.

Poppy Poppy-head tea used to be drunk to inspire visions of the faery realm, but the plant is now widely outlawed because of its opium content. You could use the seeds to decorate faery cakes (see page 119).

Primrose Wild primroses indicate the presence of faeries. Grow them to attract faeries to your home, but be sure to tend them well.

Ragwort Elves and other faeries use ragwort stalks for flying, like witches use broomsticks.

Red campion Sacred to Puck, this plant is used in faery garlands.

Rosemary Also known as elf leaf, grow it to attract elves to your home.

Thyme Faeries love the smell of thyme. Wear some as an amulet to help you see faeries. The flower buds are an ingredient of faery ointment.

Vervain A sacred, protective plant, loved by good faeries. When added to bath water, it can inspire dreams of faeryland.

Faery Trees

rituals & recipes

All trees have their own deva, and old, distinguished trees may harbor many other spirits. Elves use certain old, hollow trees as portals between the faery realm and the world of humans. Here is a list of some favorite faery trees.

Alder Red, green, and brown dyes are derived from different parts of the tree, symbolizing fire, water, and earth. The white wood turns red when cut, and is associated with dryads' blood. It is said that the protective faeries of the alder can assume the shape of a raven.

Apple Sacred to Diana, goddess of the little people. Burn the bark in honor of the faery folk on Midsummer Eve (June 22nd in the northern hemisphere; December 22nd in the southern hemisphere).

Ash The most sacred tree of the Norse peoples and a favorite tree of elves. Where ash trees grow closely together, faeries dwell. Together with oak and hawthorn, it forms the faery triad. A twig from each protects against malicious night spirits if bound together with red thread.

Birch In Scotland, birch twigs were placed in cradles to stop babies from being stolen by faeries. Faeries' favorite mushroom, the red and white fly agaric, grows under birch.

Blackthorn Blackthorn thickets are guarded by small, hairless elves that congregate there.

Elder Sometimes called witches' trees, elder provide protection for faeries, who guard them in turn. Elderberry wine is sometimes called faery wine. It is unlucky to burn the wood.

Hawthorn A favorite tree of the little people, forming part of the faery triad along with oak and ash. A wreath of hawthorn leaves is part of the costume of Jack-in-the-green.

Hazel Faeries love hazelnuts. The flower buds are an ingredient of faery ointment (see page 117), and elves use its slender branches to make wands.

Oak One of the faery triad trees, along with hawthorn and ash. According to a traditional rhyme: "Faery folks are in old oaks."

Rowan A tree loved by faeries. Also known as witchbane, it protects against witches and malicious spirits. Rowan jelly is a favorite faery food.

Willow One of the faeries' favorite trees for making magic wands.

Glossary

Alchemy A mystical science that seeks to penetrate the most intimate secrets of nature in order to perfect both humankind and matter.

Casting a glamour Mischievous faeries sometimes "cast a glamour" over humans to make them see things that are not really there or to lead them astray.

Faery ointment A magical ointment that can be smeared on the eyelids to help humans see faeries. While some of the ingredients used in the ointment are known, the complete recipe is still a mystery.

Faery rings Circles of little mushrooms where faeries like to gather. Elves often hold revels in faery rings, whereas pixies race ponies around them and turn themselves into one of the mushrooms if spotted by humans.

Fair folk One of the popular names for faeries.

Fey herbs Plants associated with faeries.

Gallitraps See "Faery rings" above.

Holey stone A stone with a naturally bored hole in it. Looking through the hole can improve your chances of seeing faeries.

Laying a faery Discouraging the attentions of faeries.

Little people Another popular euphemism for faeries.

Shaman A person who can perceive the world of spirits and, by entering a trance, journey to the spiritual realm and communicate with its inhabitants.

Soul The immortal essence of a thing that differentiates one being from another.

Spirit *1.* A non-corporeal, soulless being. *2.* The undifferentiated life force that animates all things.

War of heaven A rebellion of angels, led by Satan, that was eventually crushed. The defeated angels were cast out of heaven into the material world. One of the possible origins of faeries is that they were lesser angels caught on the wrong side of the war and were also cast out of heaven.

Further reading

Andersen, Hans Christian *Hans Christian Andersen: The Complete Fairy Tales and Stories* Anchor, 1983

Barker, Cicely Mary *The Complete Book of the Flower Fairies* Frederick Warne, 1997

Briggs, K. M. *A Dictionary of Fairies* Penguin, 1977

Burton, Richard *The Arabian Nights: Tales from a Thousand and One Nights* Modern Library, 2001

Fox, Matthew & Sheldrake, Rupert *The Physics of Angels: Exploring the Realm Where Science and Spirit Meet* Harpers, 1997

Frazer, J. G. *The Golden Bough* Papermac, 1987

Grimm Brothers *The Complete Fairy Tales of the Brothers Grimm* Bantam, 1992

Hole, C. *A Dictionary of British Folk Customs* Paladin, 1986

Keightley, Thomas *The Fairy Mythology* Whittaker-Treacher, 1833

Lang, A. *Custom & Myth* Longmans Green, 1898

Leach, M. (ed.) *The Dictionary of Folklore* Funk & Wagnall, 1985

Lurker, Manfred *Dictionary of Gods & Goddesses, Devils & Demons* Routledge, 1989

New Larousse Encyclopedia of Mythology Hamlyn, 1968

Senior, Michael *The Illustrated Who's Who in Mythology* MacDonald Illustrated, 1985

Squire, C. *Celtic Myth & Legend, Poetry & Romance* Gresham, 1889

Williams-Ellis, Anabel *Fairies and Enchanters* Nelson, 1933

Yeats, W. B. (ed.) *Fairy & Folk Tales of the Irish Peasantry* Dover Publications, 1991

Credits

Quarto would like to acknowledge the following illustrators:

Veronica Aldous: pages 10, 11, 47, 93, 109, 116, 117

Greg Becker: pages 8/9, 15, 23, 25, 35, 41, 67, 77, 81, 89, 113

Janie Coath: pages 17, 36, 37, 51, 53, 82, 83, 87, 99, 105, 107, 120, 121

Elsa Godfrey: pages 5, 14, 16, 20, 40, 44, 54, 64, 66, 68, 72, 74, 78, 84, 90, 94, 104, 106, 112

Griselda Holderness: pages 39, 61, 73, 85, 101

Martin Jones: pages 19, 31, 45, 57, 75, 79, 91, 103, 110, 111, 118, 119

Olivia Rayner: pages 21, 28, 29, 49, 95

Rob Sheffield: pages 6/7, 26, 27, 32, 33, 55, 59, 62, 63, 65, 69, 122, 123, 124, 125

Index